EITHER/OR

EITHER/OR

The Gospel or Neopaganism

Edited by

Carl E. Braaten *and* Robert W. Jenson

William B. Eerdmans Publishing Company
Grand Rapids, Michigan

© 1995 Wm. B. Eerdmans Publishing Co.
255 Jefferson Ave. S.E., Grand Rapids, Michigan 49503

Printed in the United States of America

00 99 98 97 96 95   7 6 5 4 3 2 1

Library of Congress Cataloging-in-Publication Data

Either/or: the Gospel or neopaganism /
edited by Carl E. Braaten and Robert W. Jenson.
p.   cm.
Proceedings of a conference held in Apr. 1993 at
St. Olaf College, Northfield, Minn.
Includes bibliographical references.
ISBN 0-8028-0840-9 (alk. paper)
1. United States — Religion — 1960 — Congresses. 2. United States —
Church history — 20th century — Congresses. 3. Paganism — United States —
History — 20th century — Congresses. 4. Paganism — United States —
Controversial literature — Congresses. 5. Christianity and other
religions — Congresses. 6. Apologetics — Congresses.
I. Braaten, Carl E., 1929- . II. Jenson, Robert W.
BL2525.E42 1995
239'.9 — dc20   95-8348
CIP

Contents

Preface

Carl E. Braaten and Robert W. Jenson

*"It is high time that Christians recognize that they are con-
fronted with a new paganism. Christians have been very slow
to recognize the pagan elements in modern culture. They were
so convinced that the Western world was a Christianized world
that they could not make themselves believe that pagan forces
could exert a big influence in its midst."*

Willem A. Visser 't Hooft, former General Secretary of
the World Council of Churches.[1]

It would be easier for the church if there were a clearly visible line
between the church and repaganizing Western culture. But it has
never been that simple. Indeed, the church may be said now to be
replaying the struggles of the most ancient church, occasioned
exactly by the blurring of the line. As the second-century church
worked to appropriate and transform the philosophical and other
interpretative categories of the world to which her mission led her,
she found untransformed pagans within her own fellowship who
passed themselves off as the truly "knowing" Christians, "gnostics,"
because they excelled in such ways of thinking.

1. Willem A. Visser 't Hooft, "Evangelism in the Neo-Pagan Situation,"
International Review of Mission 65 (1976): 83.

1

As Visser 't Hooft saw, the so-called Christian nations of the West are in fact the new mission fields, which the churches cannot evangelize because they have not faced the renewed paganism that is the actual religion of those to whom the gospel must there be spoken. Moreover, pagan forms of thought and behavior just so infiltrate the churches themselves, under various guises of "spirituality," "inclusive" worship, and "evangelism" — often with the active backing of those who should be responsible for the faith's integrity.

In April 1993 the Center for Catholic and Evangelical Theology sponsored a conference to consider this situation. Held at St. Olaf College in Northfield, Minnesota, the theme was "EITHER/OR: The Gospel or Neopaganism." The first part of this title appropriates the title of one of Søren Kierkegaard's early works. The Danish prophet looked at Christian Denmark and had the audacity to ask whether New Testament Christianity in fact existed anymore. The question was rhetorical; his answer was published as *Attack on Christendom*. Kierkegaard's critique was motivated by a passion for a new birth of authentic faith, overcoming the blended Christianity established in European churches since the Enlightenment.

In the present situation of the American church, Kierkegaard's either/or takes the form of what James Hunter has taught us to call "the culture wars," as these take place also inside the church. The Center's conference was not called for those who hope to be neutral in these wars. The addresses given there do not beg for enlightened dialogue between the contending parties. They are partisan. Their acknowledged context is a deadly conflict over what evangelical, catholic, and orthodox Christians believe about the triune identity of God, salvation through Christ alone, the divine institution of the holy ministry, the oneness of the church in apostolic succession, and the great commission of our Lord to go with the gospel to all nations. In the organizations of "mainline" churches, if these convictions are not denied outright they are mingled with "alternatives" in the name of "pluralism," "multiculturalism," "feminism," and "hospitality." The addresses printed here were given as direct attacks on such betrayal.

Simultaneous to the Center's conference, coincidence provided a dramatic instance of the neopaganism the conference was called to oppose, and of its virulence within the churches. The World Council of Churches, supported by the divisions for world mission of mainline denominations (Methodist, Presbyterian, Lutheran, the United Church of Christ, and others), held a conference in Minneapolis, Minnesota, on "RE-imagining the Divine." It was supposed to be an ecumenical event for Christian women, but as a friendly reporter described it, "They were there to explore the sensual and sexual side of the divine, rooting around in contemplative and introspective interplay with God, and talking about women's daily experience of the divine in every culture as central to theology today." The conference celebrated a "second Reformation"; Luther and Calvin, it was proclaimed, could never have imagined the things these women were learning from their experience — which, to be sure, is doubtless the case.

The Sunday morning service explicitly worshiped Sophia, identified as the female face of the human psyche. (We cannot help remarking that if the participants had not been ignorant of what the original gnostic devisers of this deity in fact attributed to Sophia, they might not have been so eager — but never mind.) At a ritual of milk and honey, blessing these elements, they prayed:

> Our maker Sophia, we are women in your image: With the hot blood of our wombs we give form to new life. With the courage of our convictions we pour out lifeblood for justice. Sophia, creator God, let your milk and honey flow. . . . Our sweet Sophia, we are women in your image: with nectar between our thighs we invite a lover, we birth a child; with our warm body fluids we remind the world of its pleasures and sensations. . . . Our guide, Sophia, we are women in your image: with our moist mouths we kiss away a tear, we smile encouragement. With the honey of wisdom in our mouths, we prophesy a full humanity to all the peoples.

Whatever else is to be said of such worship, it is of course the opposite of biblical faith, an amateurish but more than sufficiently explicit reinvention of the fertility-worship of Ashtoresh and Baal, against which the faith of Israel defined itself through centuries of history with the Lord God, and for our liberation from which Christ

died. Had this been just another conference of witches and chan-
nellers in Southern California, it could be dismissed for the undis-
guised foolishness it is. But thousands of churchly women, with a
few male fellow-travelers, attended: professors of "theology," pastors, chaplains, central bureaucrats, synod and diocesan officials,
students. And it was held in a demographic center of mainline
Protestantism.

Such excitements of the "new Reformation" are symptoms of
the gnosticism that culture critic Harold Bloom discovered as the
perennial core of American religiosity. "Gnosticism . . . is now, and
always has been, the hidden religion of the United States, the
American Religion proper."[2] The hallmark of this gnosticism is
experiential religiosity divorced from dogma — and indeed from all
concern for truth. "The God of the American Religion is an experiential God, so radically within our own being as to become a
virtual identity with what is most authentic (oldest and best) in the
self."[3] Bloom is not a Christian, but he sees the contradiction
between this religion and Christianity, and the failure of the
churches, far more clearly than do many clergy and professional
theologians: "Ancient Gnosticism was an elite religion or quasi-re-
ligion; the oddity of our American Gnosis is that it is a mass phenomenon. There are tens of millions of (supposedly Christian)
Americans whose obsessive idea of spiritual freedom violates the
normative basis of historical Christianity, though they are incapable
of realizing how little they share of what once was considered
Christian doctrine."[4]

Research, whether historical or by survey, has regularly concluded that the real reason for the decline of the mainline churches
is simply lack of Christian belief. Tens of thousands of cultural
gnostics are annually welcomed into mainline congregations with
no serious attempt to instruct them. Yet more tens of thousands of
the children of these congregations grow up into the gnosticism
around them, given no clue by their pastors or congregational

2. Harold Bloom, *The American Religion* (New York: Simon and Schuster,
1992), p. 50.
3. Ibid., p. 259.
4. Ibid., p. 263.

teachers that the church has any differing convictions. No wonder that as many leave annually by the back door as enter by so promiscuous a front door.

Most recently, sociologists Johnson, Hoge, and Luidens have found that the majority of church members are "lay liberals who have no clear understanding of what Christianity is or why they are Christian. They vaguely know that it has something to do with belief in God and respect for Jesus and the Golden Rule." The churches, according to this study (among many), somehow "lost the will or the ability to teach the Christian faith and what it requires."[5] "If the mainline churches want to regain their vitality, the first step must be to address theological issues head-on."[6]

The essays in this volume are at least, perhaps, "head-on." We believe that they discuss the most crucial issues for the gospel's integrity in its encounter with "the spirits of the age," roundly termed by us "neopaganism" and "gnosticism." We were not "tens of millions" at the conference, nor are millions likely now to enrich the book's venturesome publisher. But who knows how many, who have not bowed the knee to Ashtoresh, it takes to reform the church? Finally, only God — the true God, that is — will decide the "either/or."

5. Benton Johnson, Dean R. Hoge, and Donald A. Luidens, "Mainline Churches: The Real Reason for Decline," *First Things* 31 (March 1993): 15.
6. Ibid., p. 18.

The Gospel for a Neopagan Culture

Carl E. Braaten

Definition of Terms

This essay deals specifically with the juxtaposition of "gospel" and "neopaganism." Both terms are often used so loosely that I must begin with some definitions. I will not be using the word "gospel" in the narrow sense in distinction from the Law. Thus, I will not be engaging in the exercise familiar to theologians of the Reformation tradition of drawing the proper distinction between law and gospel. Rather, I will use the word "gospel" in the broad sense of the whole message of Jesus Christ. This includes not only what Jesus personally proclaimed but what his apostles proclaimed *about* him.[1]

"Neopaganism" is a word used in highly impressionistic ways. Sometimes it is a catchall for everything opposed to Christianity. I will use the term to refer to modern variations of the ancient belief of pre-Christian mystery religions that a divine spark or seed is innate in the individual human soul. Salvation consists of liberating the divine essence from all that prevents its true self-expression. The way of salvation is to turn inward and "to get in touch with oneself," as people say today. Ernst Troeltsch, writing his monumental *The Social Teaching of the Chris-*

1. See Epitome, Article V, Formula of Concord, *The Book of Concord,* Tappert edition (Philadelphia: Fortress, 1959), p. 478.

7

tian Churches in 1912, called it "the secret religion of the educated classes."[2]

The church needs to identify and withstand all expressions of neopaganism within its own life. To that end it needs to sharpen the weapons it used in its titanic struggles against gnosticism in the early centuries. I will stress three factors absolutely essential to the gospel where the battle must be fought. The first concerns the matter of history in the gospel, the second is the nature of the gospel as kerygma, and the third is the function of dogma for the gospel. History, kerygma, and dogma — gnosticism can never tolerate any one of these three. Its appeal to experience dissolves them in the acids of its own self-assured subjectivity.

It was and is foolishness to the Greeks to believe that God would choose to embody himself in one individual human being; it was and is an insult to human dignity and pride to teach that the word of salvation must come kerygmatically from the outside — *extra nos* — and that the objective saving history of God in Jesus Christ becomes gospel only through the apostolic kerygma. It was and is an intellectual affront to assert that the dogma of the church is the gift of the Holy Spirit, and that its truth is a liberation for all who are called to teach the Christian faith with power and authority. Any theology caught in a flight from history, or from kerygma, or from dogma will be led astray into an experientialism that expects from the human soul, whether in terms of its mind, or will, or feelings, what only God can give.

The Trajectory of the Gospel

One thousand nine hundred and sixty-three years ago by our calendar a young Jewish rabbi by the name of Jesus died in Jerusalem under the authority of Pontius Pilate. He died the excruciating death of a criminal on the cross. That is an objective historical fact. Indispensable to the gospel is the fact that at the beginning of the Christian faith stands the figure of Jesus of Nazareth, his preaching

2. Ernst Troeltsch, *The Social Teaching of the Christian Churches,* trans. Olive Wyon (New York: Macmillan, 1931), 2:794.

of the kingdom of God, his intimate sense of being his Abba's Son, his way of accepting social outcasts, his table fellowship with sinners, and finally his obedient suffering and death on the cross. All that is concrete historical stuff, the granite foundation of the Christian faith.

A generation later this same person, Jesus of Nazareth, was singled out as one whom God raised from the dead. Shortly after the shocking death of this righteous rabbi from Nazareth, Jesus became the messianic subject of the missionary proclamation of the apostles. The core of the kerygma is thus a narrative of God acting — full of talk of resurrection, exaltation, and enthronement — setting in motion a rich unfolding of christological confessions of Jesus as Lord and Savior, Jesus as Messiah and Son of Man, Jesus as the Logos and Son of God. This is the christological stuff that fills the earliest apostolic kerygma.

Then about three centuries later the bishops assembled at Nicaea confessed the crucified and risen Lord Jesus Christ as "God from God, Light from Light, true God from true God, begotten not created, of the same essence as the Father." And in the middle of the next century (451 A.D.) the Council of Chalcedon coined the dogmatic formula *"vere Deus et vere homo."* This Christ, true God and true man, born of the Father before all time, in these last days is born of the Virgin Mary "for us and for our salvation." All of this is the wonderful language of doxology and dogma.

This brief sketch shows the trajectory of the gospel of God moving from the historical Jesus to the kerygmatic Christ to the dogmatic confession equating Jesus with God. The whole gospel of the church rests on this christological tripod — these three interconnected legs of history, kerygma, and dogma, of Jesus of Nazareth as the risen Lord and as God's only begotten Son. When one of these legs is removed, broken, or shortened in the life, worship, and witness of the church, the door of hospitality opens to pagan spirituality and alien ideology. This is what is happening in American Christianity today and in some trends of theology.

One conspicuous trend is to debunk christocentric theology in favor of a theocentrism that places God at the center of the universe of faiths, relegating Christ to one among many ways of enlightenment, liberation, and salvation. This theocentric pluralism appears in the theological ethics of James Gustafson, in the feminist theology of Rosemary Radford Ruether and many other feminists, and in the pluralistic theory of religions of John Hick and Paul Knitter. They portray Jesus as the founder of one of the great religions whose symbols and rituals point to the quintessential unity in the depths of ultimate reality. Christians project their favorite metaphors on the blank tablet of the anonymous mystery at the heart of the universe, and other religions do it their way just as well. These theologies have no gospel whatsoever because their Jesus is dead, not the risen Lord of the apostolic kerygma and God-Man of ecclesial dogma.

Liberal Protestant theology has always limped along with a defective Christology, especially in America. After his visit to the United States, Dietrich Bonhoeffer remarked:

> The rejection of Christology is characteristic of the whole of present-day American theology. Christianity basically amounts to religion and ethics in American theology. Consequently, the person and work of Christ fall into the background and remain basically not understood in this theology.[3]

Yet there is no lack of Jesuology; American religion of all kinds retains its fascination with Jesus, as one of the most unforgettable personalities of all time. But there can be no real gospel-bearing Christology, none that can support the weight of human bondage and the freight of the world's salvation, minus the kerygma of the risen Lord and minus the dogma of the only begotten Son of God.

The theologian who classically epitomizes a Christianity of the historical Jesus apart from the apostolic kerygma and the ecclesial dogma is Adolf von Harnack. I say "epitomizes" because Harnack was the greatest among the Protestant theologians who tried to refound Christianity on the results of a purely historical reconstruction of its origins. He was perched at the summit of two hundred years of historical scientific work from H. S. Reimarus and G. E. Lessing to F. C. Baur and D. F. Strauss, whose aim was to rediscover

---

3. Dietrich Bonhoeffer, "Protestantismus ohne Reformation," in *Gesammelte Schriften,* ed. Eberhard Bethge (Munich: Chr. Kaiser Verlag, 1958), p. 352.

the Jesus of history as he really was prior to the preaching of the apostles and the dogmatic interpretations of the fathers and councils of the church.

Forty years ago when I began in earnest to study theology, the theological climate was not favorable to Harnack's liberal theology. First Martin Kähler and then Albert Schweitzer had signaled that the quest of the historical Jesus was a very dubious affair, and then Karl Barth and the dialectical theologians in general suggested that christologically we can somehow do an end-run around the historical-critical approach to the Jesus of the Gospels. After all, the liberals had given the historical Jesus of critical scholarship a bad reputation. Should that not give us a license to move away from history to the kerygmatic Christ of Paul and the apostles and perhaps even to the dogmatic Christ of the creeds and the fathers?

But after a generation of kerygmatic and dogmatic Christology, following the lead of Rudolf Bultmann and Karl Barth, history would not be denied its due. Käsemann and Bornkamm in New Testament studies and then Pannenberg in systematic theology took a step back into history, back to the history of Jesus within the kerygma and preceding the dogma, as a protest against what they called "docetism." In some sense the historical Jesus must always remain the necessary starting point of Christology. Prior to Christianity, before there was ever such a thing as Christology, there was Jesus of Nazareth. It was precisely in him that the Word became flesh. With the rise of the so-called "new quest of the historical Jesus," the conviction prevailed that both kerygma and dogma without history become vulnerable to docetism, the child of gnosticism.

Many theologians of my generation struggled to construct an adequate Christology faithful to the original gospel, on the one hand, and responsive to contemporary questions, on the other hand. We worked our way through the monumental thought patterns of two giants, Rudolf Bultmann and Karl Barth. Bultmann allied himself with Barth in the early days in the interest of a theology of the Word of the transcendent God who encounters humanity from beyond. For both Barth and Bultmann theology is possible only in light of the Word of God, the Christ-event. Bultmann took up his program of demythologizing for the sake of the kerygma — to make sure that nothing but the kerygma would be preached today, and not the obsolete husks of a mythical worldview. But when all the dust had settled, it became clear that Bultmann's kerygmatic Christology had lost its history, the history of Jesus of Nazareth, and in its place Bultmann poured in statements from his own existential self-understanding as a Christian, shaped by existentialist philosophy. A kerygma without history became captive to a philosophy of existence — which for many intellectuals devoted to Martin Heidegger or Karl Jaspers had become a substitute for Christian faith. Bultmann had reacted so radically against the historical Jesus of Harnack's liberal theology that he was ready to abandon everything except the bare paradox that the Word became flesh and died on the cross. Even the question whether his name was "Jesus" was merely a matter of historical interest, and of no essential concern to the Christian faith.

Bultmann's flight from history threw open the gate to accommodate an existentialist form of gnosticism, as Hans Jonas made unmistakably clear. The clearest examples can be seen in the theologies of Fritz Buri and Schubert Ogden. For these liberal theologians the Christ-event is a mere symbol of authentic existence, not the necessary condition of its possibility.[4] The *solus Christus* of the gospel to which Bultmann clung has evaporated into existential self-understanding.

Today we are witnessing a renewal of interest in the historical Jesus. The new pictures of the historical Jesus, such as those in Marcus Borg, Dominic Crosson, John P. Meier, A. N. Wilson, John Spong, or Robert Funk's Jesus-Seminar, are constructed (as was Harnack's) as if Jesus' own history had come to a stop with his death on the cross, as if the apostolic kerygma and ecclesial dogma did not provide definitive disclosures of the identity of Jesus, but were somewhat arbitrary embellishments of his meaning imaginatively constructed by later believers for their own purposes.

Harnack formulated the gospel for liberal Protestantism in his famous saying: "The gospel, as Jesus proclaimed it, has to do with the Father only and not with the Son."[5] This Jesuological gospel

4. See Schubert Ogden's introduction to *Existence and Faith: Shorter Writings of Rudolf Bultmann,* trans. Schubert M. Ogden (New York: Meridian Books, 1960), p. 20.

5. Adolf von Harnack, *What is Christianity?* trans. T. B. Saunders (New York: Harper & Brothers, 1957), p. 144.

has now returned as the centerpiece of the new theocentric pluralists who cannot say that Christ is God, but only that God was in Christ, not exclusively in a categorically unique sense, but inclusively along with other saints, sages, and founders of world religions. As much as we must oppose this reductionistic return to the historical Jesus that proceeds apart from the later kerygmatic and dogmatic confessions and hermeneutics of the church, we cannot dispense with the fact that Jesus of Nazareth is himself both the ground and content of the gospel, and that without him we have no specifically Christian doctrine of God.

Karl Barth was a devoted student of Harnack in Berlin. He quickly saw that Harnack's historical-critical reconstruction of the history of Jesus was a prisoner of the bourgeois mindset of liberal academic Christianity. Harnack investigated the origins of Christianity and became mired in the relativities of history, from which one can derive no certainties. Barth broke through to the transcendent origin of all reality and addressed the eternal Word of God from beyond history to the crises of this age.

However, Barth was just as disinterested as Bultmann was in the historical personality of Jesus in the sense of liberal theology. For Barth Jesus Christ *is* the eternal Word of God, the divine Son born of the Father before all time. Unlike Bultmann, who tried to keep his balance sitting on a one-legged stool — only on the kerygma — Barth rediscovered the christological and trinitarian dogmas of the fathers of the ancient church, the ecumenical councils, and Protestant orthodoxy. With Barth, Christology acquired a second leg, not only kerygma but also dogma. Jesus is none other than the eternal Logos in the flesh. Barth said, contra the liberals, "Because Jesus is the Logos, the Word of God become flesh (*not* because of the man in himself), we apprehend God in the man Jesus. . . . There is no person Jesus existing apart from the Logos."[6] If God reveals himself through the Logos and the Logos is Jesus, the one who reveals God can hardly be less than God. Here Barth frames the kerygma of the crucified and risen Jesus with the dogma of the

6. Karl Barth, "The Principles of Dogmatics according to Wilhelm Herrmann," in *Theology and Church,* trans. Louise Pettibone Smith (New York: Harper & Row, 1962), p. 264.

Godhead of Jesus Christ. Here in this concrete God-man, here in the divine-human person of Jesus Christ, we have the heart of the gospel and the center of the Bible.

After Barth and Bultmann, theology found it necessary to return to the historical question — starting a new quest of the historical Jesus. Such a new quest can be conducted on the premises of a naturalistic, rationalistic, or positivistic interpretation of history, or on any other premises, Marxist, Freudian, or Nietzschean. So why not proceed on presuppositions shaped by the kerygma and dogma of the church? Why should the church and its theologians borrow their premises from the neopagan elements at the base of Enlightenment modernity?

Liberal theology has no right to a monopoly on the historical Jesus. Christology that ignores the concrete life of the Word made flesh in space and time comes too close to docetism and the gnostic flight from history. Our interest in the Jesus of history, in the *humanity* of God incarnate, is not irrelevant to faith. There can be no real Christology without the eschatological prophet from Nazareth, his own relation to the Jewish people and to their God, his teachings, his miracles, and his attitudes toward others.

Ernst Käsemann well expressed my conviction concerning the trajectory of the gospel when he wrote:

> For two hundred years, critical research has been trying to free the Jesus of history from the fetters of the church's dogma, only to find at the end that such an attempt was predestined to failure, and that we can learn nothing at all about the historical Jesus except through the medium of primitive Christian preaching and of the church's dogma which is bound up with it. We can no longer detach him neatly and satisfactorily from the Christ of preaching and of faith.[7]

Christology adequate for the gospel's encounter with neopaganism is a three-legged stool. Both kerygma and dogma have a life-and-death stake in the historicity of God's revelation in Jesus Christ. Harnack's gospel is an example of history without kerygma

---

7. Ernst Käsemann, "The Problem of the Historical Jesus," in *Essays on New Testament Themes,* trans. W. J. Montague (London: SCM, 1964), p. 17.

and dogma. Bultmann's kerygma languishes in abstraction from history and dogma. Barth's Christology combines kerygma and dogma with remarkable indifference to historical questions.

The Hidden Legacy of Paganism

The outcome of the encounter of the gospel with our neopagan culture will be decided by the strength of our Christology. Many current Christologies are trying to equip the church for its mission today without the resurrection of Jesus and the divinity of Christ, thus deficient both as kerygma and dogma. Karl Barth saw the folly of liberal Christology in contrast to orthodox Christology.

> Orthodox Christology is a glacial torrent rushing straight down from a height of three thousand metres; it makes accomplishment possible. Herrmann's Christology, as it stands, is the hopeless attempt to raise the stagnant pool to that same height by means of a hand pump; nothing can be accomplished with it.[8]

The neopaganism we are contending with is a reemergence of the pagan elements of Western civilization. They entered American religion through the founding fathers of our democracy. Thomas Jefferson wrote, "Do we want to know what God is? Search not the book called Scripture, which any human hand might make, but the scripture called creation."[9] David Gill says that "Jefferson spent part of his life editing out forty-six pages of 'acceptable' parts of Jesus' teaching from the Gospels. What was left he called the most sublime and benevolent code of morals which has ever been offered to man."[10] Jefferson was not the last to produce a bowdlerized Scripture to suit his own agenda. Contemporary lectionaries read in our churches every Sunday are doing the same abominable thing with the support of many bishops, pastors, and theologians.

8. Barth, "Principles of Dogmatics," p. 265.
9. Cited in David Gill, "The Faith of the Founding Fathers," in *One Nation Under God* (Waco, Tex.: Word Books, 1975), p. 41.
10. Ibid., p. 42.

America is founded on a creed, but it is the creed of the Enlightenment, not the Christian creed. Many conservative American Christians are so convinced that America was born a Christian nation that they cannot believe that its present inhospitality to Christianity is a phenomenon profoundly rooted in our origins. We need to debunk this widespread "myth of Christian beginnings" (Robert Wilken) before the churches will recognize that they face the challenge of old-fashioned paganism underlying the dominant thought forms in education, business, jurisprudence, medicine, science, entertainment, and the arts.

But this is nothing new. Western civilization never was Christian to its core. The history of the West has been a syncretism of various streams of religious symbols. When Christianity became the established religion of the West, it provided a general glaze covering up the virility of pagan culture lying below the surface. The Greek ideal was humanistic. Again and again the humanistic image of society erupted in the midst of Christianity — at the time of the Renaissance, the Enlightenment, nineteenth-century socialism, and twentieth-century Marxist revolutionary ideology. These movements emerged in the West as rivals of the Christian faith, and they were nourished by a vision of human dignity and destiny embedded in the culture of ancient Greece. In this system of values, humanity is at the center; "man is the measure of all things," as Protagoras said. During the flowering of Greek culture a shift took place from the realm of the gods to the world of human beings. Greek art, religion, political thought, and science were based on the values of ideal humanity, on the ideal human community, on humanistic concepts of beauty, liberty, virtue, truth, and justice. Greek culture provided a prototype of all succeeding humanistic images of human being and community that periodically erupted in the not so Christian West. As much as there is to love and admire in this vision, it stands in polar opposition to the Hebraic-Christian vision rooted in the revelation of Israel's God.

The spiritual riches of Greece spread in ever-widening circles through the whole Mediterranean world. The utopia of the ideal state lived on in the Hellenistic world empire of Alexander the Great, representing a vision of an ideal reign of peace. This vision of an ideal earthly city lived on in the Roman Empire, which in its turn influenced European thought for centuries to come. In addition to Greece, then, the Roman Empire left its stamp on the budding young faith.

In the Middle Ages images of human nature and destiny from pagan sources in Iran, Greece, and Rome were like sticks of dynamite with the potential to blow up the Roman Catholic empire. Seeds were sown that later produced anti-Christian movements in the Renaissance, English deism, the French Revolution, the German Enlightenment, and romanticism. The humanistic thrust of the Renaissance was extended into the age of the Enlightenment, taking a number of anti-churchly turnings.

Christian apologetics tried to accommodate every new apostasy with the consolation that the new pagans were only experimenting with novel ways of being Christian. This kind of apologetics, however, leads the way to the idea of "unconscious Christianity" (Rothe), "anonymous Christians" (Rahner), and the "latent church" (Tillich). The German encyclopedia *Religion in Geschichte und Gegenwart* (1913) ended its article on Goethe by declaring him to be the first representative of the Christianity of the future — a strange thing to say in view of the fact that Goethe declared himself to be decidedly a non-Christian. This is hardly less embarrassing than hailing Thomas Jefferson, as one historian has done, as the "St. Paul of American democracy," in spite of the fact that Jefferson despised the apostle as the corrupter of the pure moral teachings of Jesus.

The circle of neopaganism has been closing in on Christianity for a long time. The intellectual history of England cannot be told without recording the outbreakings of deism, empiricism, and positivism; in France materialism, pantheism, and atheism; in Germany rationalism, naturalism, and romanticism. Add to these the twentieth-century movements of Marxism, existentialism, and nihilism, and we have a partial list of labels that denote something of the breadth and depth of the apostasies rising up against the church and the Christian faith. All of them have found free room to roam across the intellectual landscape of the American academy, and alongside each one there is sure to be a theologian or bishop ready to pronounce a benediction in the name of the gospel. No wonder that Nietzsche could scream out, "God is dead," which we can take to mean that Christians have so compromised the gospel that their churches have become like tombs for the God they have buried.

Christianity in America Today

In conclusion I want to touch on some of the flash points of the encounter of the gospel and neopaganism within Christianity today. We have no precise model to follow. Some recent books on Christianity in America today suggest that the churches are in utter confusion about what to do. These include Philip J. Lee's *Against the Protestant Gnostics*, Robert Wuthnow's *The Struggle for America's Soul*, Harold Bloom's *The American Religion,* James Davison Hunter's *Culture Wars*, and Mark R. Schwehn's *Exiles From Eden*. They all document that the churches are conspicuously unsure of what it means to be church, that is, the community defined by its worship of Christ as the revelation of the triune God, where the Gospel stories of Jesus are read, where the kerygma of God's eschatological act in Christ is preached, where baptized believers commune with the risen Lord, and where Jesus' saving power and identity with God is publicly confessed.

The denominations that claim to be church are in thrall to theological ideas, moral values, and social practices emanating from contemporary post-Christian culture rather than from its own revelation-based doctrines and traditions. Some theologies apply a "hermeneutic of suspicion" to the entire sweep of the Christian tradition, including the Bible. Churches are selling their souls to the highest bidders, attracting consumers with a product whose appeal is success not faithfulness, self-esteem not discipleship, techniques not truth. Christian higher education, colleges and seminaries, bought into the Enlightenment model of separating knowledge from Christian truth, of stressing research at the expense of shaping moral character.

The theology of the cross has been replaced by a theology of glory — just what the gnostics always wanted. If the aim of the church is to grow, the way to do it is to make people feel good. And when people discover that there are other ways to feel good, they leave the church they no longer need. The relevant church is sowing the seeds of its own irrelevance, and losing its identity to boot. The big question today has become how to get the baby boomers back, what techniques and methods will do the trick. Polls are taken on what baby boomers want and churches are competing to make sure they get it.

The predictions of the secular theologians of some decades ago have proved all wrong. "Modern man" was supposed to be completely secular, with no feeling for mystery, myth, and magic, no need for transcendence and inwardness, no anxieties about guilt, sin, and death. The religious dimensions of life are supposedly passé in a "world come of age." Today the polls tell us that Westerners and Americans, to the contrary, are very religious, that they are long on *believing* but short on *belonging.* They will believe almost anything but belong to nothing that calls for lifelong commitment, obedience to authority, an ethic of self-denial, discipline, and sacrifice.

Let the church be the church! If the church must decrease so that Christ must increase, let it be. The church is not free to be a megachurch at all cost. The church is not free to cultivate a spirituality of self-fulfillment. The church is not free to entertain every novel hermeneutic of Scripture. The church is not free to invoke the ancestral spirits at home in aboriginal religions or pray to the goddesses of the ancient mystery-cults. The church's dogma forbids it. That is what the dogma is for, to prevent paganism from entering the "holy of holies" where the worship of Christ erupts into the praise of the triune God.

Let us be clear about this. Neopaganism does not mean no religion at all. It means a different religion — a "different gospel." And usually it appears not in naked form but quite often dressed in Christian symbols that fool the masses. Even Christ is welcome in the gnostic pantheon, but not necessarily as Jesus, only as an empty vessel into which each age pours its own ideals and values. The sole function of Jesus is to stimulate the religious consciousness.

Neopaganism is spiritual religion attuned to the "Zeitgeist." It has no use for the concrete historical element of the biblical gospel. It has no need of the church and the external word *(verbum externum),* turning instead to pure immediacy and inwardness in which each individual personally acquires knowledge of God out of the depths of his or her own experience. People of this type care solely for their own spiritual journeys through life, and while they believe in an emerging universal fellowship in the spirit of love, the reality of the church as an elect communion of saints and sacred things is alien to their thinking. They do not understand the doctrines of the gospel to be true statements about events that have happened once for all, but see them as symbols of eternal truths reflecting ever-recurrent processes of life in the presence of God. History itself is nothing but a resource of symbols to stimulate certain moods and feelings according to each person's private fancy. Worship means getting together in small groups of kindred spirits to hear one another's stories.

Evangelical pietism that has lost the catholic elements of the great tradition provides a fertile soil for such ahistorical spiritual religion. There are signs that American evangelicalism with its pietist background is breaking up under the impact of the "culture wars," with one wing seeking to reattach itself to catholic and orthodox traditions, which we welcome, and the other wing allying itself opportunistically with the culture-conforming progressives in American religion.[11]

A gospel-centered counteroffensive will not work without the kind of full-orbed Christology I have proposed. Such a Christology is not an abstract piece of speculative dogmatics. The historical, kerygmatic, and dogmatic components of the gospel equip the church to stake its entire life on Christ, leaving no place for any other love or loyalty. This and nothing else will immunize the church against anthropocentric theologies of experience. Only such a christologically anchored gospel will keep the church from becoming a multiplicity of religious sects drifting away from the original source from which the energies of faith flow.

I am unable here to draw out the implications for the church's life, witness, and mission of such a christologically anchored sense of the gospel. There are, however, definite implications for the liturgies of the church, for its language and forms, for preaching and counseling, for catechesis and biblical interpretation, for the

---

11. See, e.g., *Power Religion: The Selling Out of the Evangelical Church?* ed. Michael Scott Horton, with essays by Charles Colson, J. I. Packer, R. C. Sproul, Alister McGrath, and others (Chicago: Moody, 1992).

spiritual formation and education of pastors, for the dominically instituted ministry of the church and its historic structures of authority and administration, for the universal mission of the gospel and its hope for the world. With a low Christology the implications are exceedingly thin and optional; with a high Christology the implications are thick and compelling.

The God-Wars

Robert W. Jenson

This essay will be primarily about the culture in which the church finds itself, and only indirectly about the church as such. The title is, of course, a parody of the title of a recent book about the "culture-wars," a title that has quickly become a slogan much in use by commentators. And the slogan undoubtedly points to something real in American life; we have all experienced these wars in our communities and congregations. We fight about photographic exhibitions, school curricula, homosexuality, abortion, pluralism, the place of religion in public life, euthanasia — the list goes on and on. Yet when the slogan is used for more analytic purposes, it often fails us. The slogan surely indicates a trouble, but does not seem reliably to promote understanding of what the trouble is. What exactly are we fighting over? That will be the burden of my essay.

A notable feature of America's cultural battles is the multiplicity of implausible alliances and truces. Old-fashioned rationalists and new-age mystagogues have no public worries about each other, though both worry much about the lamentably sectarian views of practicing Jews or Christians. Gender feminists and predatory males join hands to fortify abortion clinics against an almost equally surprising league of Catholic bishops and Baptist populists. The Republican Party depends about evenly on evangelical Christians and amoralist libertarians. And so on and on.

I suggest that we look at this scene as at the current Balkan

23

disasters. There the forming and reforming alliances sort themselves out once we realize that in one or another way they all shape themselves to a single pole, the unredeemed memory of the Ottoman empire. In the present case the swirl of cultural storms has a cyclonic center: the memory of cultural authority exercised by the biblical God, the God of Abraham. We are at war about culture just insofar as culture is the body of religion.

It has finally come to this: After centuries of love-hate between biblical religion and the Western civilization it has enabled and regularly perturbs, we are increasingly pressed to be either for the Lord or against him. So long as Christianity was normative in the culture and society, with Judaism as a sort of backup, Americans could rely on the Lord's ordinances without commitment to his cause. Now many who supposed they were for him line up practically on the other side; many who thought themselves serenely beyond religious concerns are revealed as lifelong zealous opposers. It even happens that some who thought themselves apostate rally to what is in fact his cause.

Our conflicts, I propose, are about the biblical God. Evidence for diagnoses of this kind is inevitably at once anecdotal and sweepingly generalizing. I can at most try to make my diagnosis plausible by setting some phenomena in its light, so that readers may see if they then appear more well-defined. A not very systematically chosen set of cases follows. I will try to describe the sides accurately, but will make no pretense of neutrality.

The Ideology of Pluralism

A first phenomenon is the just-mentioned ideology of pluralism, now in nearly total control of the academy and of the legal, religious, and publicistic bureaucracies. Pluralism itself, of course, is simply a permanent fact that we may applaud, deplore, or maybe even evaluate in some more analytic fashion. The world is full of religions and yogas and ideologies, and always has been and been known to be so. Often enough, these are irreconcilable: One could hardly, for classic example, simultaneously have obeyed the God who rescued Israel from Egypt and the pantheon who tried to keep her there. The presence of contrary faiths and practices within a society often causes formidable problems, as America now experiences with unwonted intensity but as has always been the case. With due respect to some pop theologians, none of this is newly discovered: Isaiah or St. Paul knew more about the theory and practice of a religiously and ideologically plural world than do all the seminary and religion faculties of California.

The *ideology* of pluralism is, however, quite another matter — though it too is old, as old as late antique civilization. Pluralism as ideology is a rule for deciding what ideas or practices, besides pluralism itself, are to be approved. Tolerable ideas and practices are those that lead us unreservedly to applaud the fact of pluralism, and good ones are those that actively promote the proliferation of pluralism both factual and ideological.

To understand the situation in which the rule of this ideology puts us, we must first note one of its chief and excruciatingly ironic effects: It silences a lot of people. The more pluralist the ideology that rules, the less are certain convictions admitted to the public arena. This has often been noticed, also — and only sometimes with embarrassment at the irony — by those who espouse the ideology.

The more interesting observation, however, is made when we go on to ask *who* in fact is silenced and *when,* and what sorts of speech are offensive within the discourse of ideological pluralism. So far as my observation reaches, the silenced are almost always those who if they spoke would say something characteristically Jewish or Christian or Islamic. Try, for example, arguing that unrestricted permission to abort the unborn is a social and political evil at a party in Manhattan or a college town in Minnesota. Your arguments will not be rebutted; heads will merely be turned as from one who has audibly broken wind. If, on the other hand, you argue what is in fact the *conventional* opinion, you will be praised for courage and compassion. Or relate two conversions, one to Christianity and the other away from it; one will be received as a tale of horrid narrow-mindedness and the other as an example of an open society's marvelous possibilities.

Last November nearly the whole roster of essayists for this volume attended the national meeting of the American Academy of Religion in San Francisco. The AAR is administered by the most ideologically pluralist guild of them all, the college and university teachers of "religious studies." One would expect all views to be permitted at such a gathering, and a superficial glance at the immense catalogue of papers might seem to confirm the expectation: If "The Nipple and the Native: The Story of the Colon-izing Apocalypse" does not attract, perhaps "Undoing Ethics/Ethics' Undoing: Irigary's Post-Lacanian Psychoanalytic Critique of Normative Discourse . . ." will. The world's smorgasbord of nonbiblical religions and substitutes for religion is laid out, and if no existing religion or religion-substitute appeals, one will be cooked or synthesized to taste. But close observation of the bars and lobbies will discover wandering loners and little knots of dissidents who apparently find little to do in the official program. Introduce yourself, and you will meet the Christian theologians whose predecessors once created the organization.

This assymetry has a simple explanation: Judaism, Christianity, and Islam are in fact disruptive of the discourse shaped by pluralist ideology and so will naturally be ejected if possible. To be sure, Judaism and Christianity have through most of their multicultural histories lived perfectly well in religiously and ideologically plural situations, and some have even argued that the West's unique creation of political and social structures to accommodate such pluralism has depended on their influence. But the *ideology* of pluralism must nevertheless — or perhaps in part just for that reason — see the Abrahamic religions as inimical.

Christianity and Islam are missionary religions which hold that their message is true for all. Judaism expects all nations finally to assemble at Zion for worship of its particular God. Each, moreover, resists the penetration of pluralism into its own community: Most of Israel's Scripture is devoted to the record of the Lord's struggle against his people's worship of other gods; Christianity can know "no other name"; and Islam can acknowledge no rival prophet.

The problem with the God of Abraham is that he is definitively the "jealous God." He has invariably refused to join whatever pantheon was going; just and only for that reason, his adherents have been persecuted. He is an outsider among deities in that he does not regard religion as necessarily a good thing, or all gods therefore as colleagues. To the contrary, his salvation is precisely rescue from humankind's general religious propensities. To honor him, therefore, *is* to renounce other candidates for deity: "I am 'the Lord,' your God; you shall have no others." Understandably, those who want to worship all gods as one cannot tolerate this one God.

Fundamentalism

A fascinating and diagnostic if perhaps minor phenomenon is the current media alarm about "fundamentalism." Pundits who concur in nothing else use "fundamentalist" as an unquestioned pejorative, and apparently possess clear marks by which to recognize the evil where it appears. In the picture presented by the public newsprints and broadcasts, Christian fundamentalists threaten to defile American politics with sectarian conflicts, Jewish fundamentalists hinder the Mideastern peace process, and Islamic fundamentalists replace Communists as all-purpose bogey-persons.

There do not, however, seem to be Buddhist or "Native-American spirituality" or Bahai or animist or Taoist fundamentalists about (although recently "Hindu fundamentalists" have appeared; I will come to them in a bit). Nor, in Columbus's recent year of reproach, were Aztec fundamentalists discovered to match the Christian fundamentalists Columbus evidently smuggled in steerage, even though the worship of Huitzlopochtli — what with state monopoly and a diet of blood — would seem admirably designed to produce illiberal types. How is that?

Undoubtedly there are accurately so-called *Christian* fundamentalists. These are the followers of an American school of theologians and church leaders who around the turn of the century identified, in response to perceived threats to the faith, a list of five "fundamental" doctrines as distinguished from others based on them. But one wonders if those who worry about "fundamentalists" have exactly these people in mind. How many columnists have the list of five doctrines at the ready, so as to tell, for example, fundamental Baptists from conservative Baptists of other schools?

The notion of *Jewish* fundamentalism stretches a good bit further, since Judaism is not first defined by doctrines. Nevertheless, in consequence of American Judaism's assimilation to the pattern of American denominationalism, the idea has a certain analogical plausibility, if little actual application.

But whatever would an *Islamic* fundamentalist be — in the commentaries and news releases the very worst and most prevalent kind? Islam has a rigorously simple message: "There is no God but God and Muhammad is his prophet." How are fundamentals and nonfundamentals to be distinguished here? Talk of Islamic fundamentalism finally betrays what the speakers are doing. The phrase "Islamic fundamentalists" turns out, on inspection of its use, to denote Muslims who discountenance the existence of a society or state independent of God's will, who find God's will stated in Quran and Sharia, and who therefore think that the state should conform society to Quran and Sharia. But this is the definition simply of a Muslim; "Islam" *means* universal individual and collective submission to God's will.

"Fundamentalist" Muslims, then, are just integral or reintegrating Muslims: followers of the Prophet who have not been captured by the cultural imperialism of the modern West, or are trying to recover from such captivity, and who therefore do not approve a wall between church and state, absolute individual autonomy, and other Western Enlightenment principles. Were not pluralist ideology what it hiddenly is, pluralists would love them for their differences from us.

Talk about "Islamic fundamentalism" is all too transparently a way of deploring Islam itself without appearing to do so — the appearance of course would be shaming, since in America Islam is still exotic and therefore is not fair game. The prevalence of the scam poses two questions. Why do we want to denounce Islam? And why is the word "fundamentalist" apt to do this, covertly? The answer to both questions is — again transparently — the same. Actual Muslims do something alarming so blatantly that it cannot be overlooked: They take the will of God seriously, and as the will of a living reality with his own ideas and universal authority to achieve them. Among American Christians, the fundamentalists are now the only ones who do the same and are known by our religiously uninformed public elites to do so. Since some Jews seem to take God seriously — those who wear yarmulkes or stranger items — there must be Jewish fundamentalists also. It comes to this: "fundamentalists" are those who reckon with the biblical God as a moral reality in and of his own self.

But what then of the new Hindu "fundamentalists"? This apparent counterexample is surely the strangest usage of all, since Hinduism has no doctrines whatever. Use of "Hindu fundamentalists" in the media turns out to refer to Indian nationalist revanchists: Rather like the Serbs, they are still enraged by past Islamic invasion and regard descendants of the invaders and their converts as traitors. It appears that "fundamentalist" has in this use finally come to mean someone who does irrational and socially dangerous things and invokes religion in the doing.

One may indeed wonder why anyone would suppose "fundamentalist," of all words, apt to deliver this judgment, since the original and meaningfully so-called American Protestant fundamentalists have been notably devoted to civic order and to a rigorous practice of reason. An answer suggests itself: The word is used in this fashion by persons who so confusedly fear the only serious religion they know that they transfer the aversion to serious religion at large.

However this last may be, it is worshipers of the God of Abraham who are normally suspected of "fundamentalism." This is no accident. It characterizes this God that he must be taken seriously for his own will and purpose, or not at all. Thus according to Judaism and Christianity, he chose Israel because he decided to, though she was "the least of the nations" and not very apparently willing to be chosen. According to Christianity, he raised his servant Jesus to be Lord of all, though the career and fate of this prophet and rabbi were a scandal to Jews and foolishness to Gentiles. According to Islam, he sent messages by a militant desert Arab, which has indeed proven a worry for the rest of us. Whatever is he up to? By *any* account of his history, his actions follow no scenario we would devise.

If God is this God, then God is God independently of us, and is not the metaphorically projected confirmation of our dreams or *ressentiment;* then Ludwig Feuerbach and Mary Daly and Oral Roberts and Matthew Fox and Robert Schuller and the central officials of nearly all denominations have it backward. If God is this God, then we cannot control him to our wishes, and "how I feel about God" or "the kind of God I need" is beside any point at all; then we must *reckon* with God. America's publicistic elites are understandably frightened by this God, and ward him off by calling his worshipers what they think is a bad name.

Abortion

Next in my selection of conflicts must be the struggle over abortion — much as one might wish to avoid it. The alliances in this case are not merely strange, they are bizarre.

Consider the last Democratic national convention. Suppose that a Martian visitor arrived whose only knowledge about abortion in America was that it is permitted more or less on demand and that the permission is controversial between "pro-choice" and "pro-life" factions. Such a visitor, hearing the rhetoric of Clinton's and Gore's speeches about the defense of the defenseless and similar topics, must infallibly have concluded that here was a convocation of the pro-life faction. Among earthlings, who know the contrary, some of us for just that reason believed none of the rhetoric. Or however did the Republicans, always sentimental for governmental nonintervention, come to be the last refuge of those who indeed want government present in the consulting room and its sanctions even in the bedroom?

It is not in fact difficult for reason to discover what would be a just legal regulation of abortion, or anyway what would not be. If I may use the trivial example of myself, it did not take divine revelation to show the error of my once pro-choice opinions. I was asked to give a speech, to prepare for which I had to read *Roe v. Wade*. It was an embarrassing experience. And I quickly came to a new personal hypothesis: that any position was unlikely to be right that had to be defended among its most able advocates with such manifestly question-begging and broken-backed reasoning.

Moreover, *Roe* itself imposed on me a valid and sufficient argument against permitting abortion on anything remotely like demand. The justices had it right at the beginning of their decision, and their position is confirmed by every new bit of embryological information: There is no plausible way to draw a temporal line before which we can know that the fetus is not a human person deserving legal protection from vendetta and after which we can know that she is. But what follows is plainly the opposite of the justices' conclusion. For the fetus certainly *will* one day be a person deserving the protection of law, and if at any given time we cannot know that she is not yet such a person, what we do not at that time know is any justification for treating her as other than one.

Yet what I of course discovered when I gave the speech, and through the years as I have been drawn intermittently into the public debate, is that reasoning has in this matter no effect at all. When abortion is the matter at issue, the most transparently valid and materially stringent argument is simply not apprehended by folk otherwise able to come in from the rain or do their own taxes. Why is that?

The mystery is uncovered if we concentrate on the slogan of the one party: They are exactly "pro-*choice.*" Pro-life attempts to call their opponents pro-abortionists, as if being pro-abortion were worse than being pro-choice, are misguided. The decision whether or not to abort is indeed a choice uniquely important for the pregnant woman; and merely *therefore* it must, according to the devisers and defenders of present law, be in her individual sole discretion. That is the whole and singular argument and position, and no other considerations are allowed to count against its force. What is in fact at stake for those who demand a right to abort at will is the understanding and practice of individual choice itself as the ultimate value of life, superseding even justice and even justice in a lethal matter, if it comes to that.

The more recent Supreme Court decision, *Planned Parenthood v. Casey,* makes the point very clear indeed. The majority opinion in *Casey* recognized that the court's arguments in *Roe* itself were feeble, and concentrated the whole defense of "the essential holding of *Roe*" on one single point: the "substantive liberty" of the pregnant woman. The court's new majority defined this with the greatest imaginable extremity: "the heart of liberty is the right to define one's own concept of existence, of meaning, of the universe, and of the mystery of human life." Exercise of this amazing freedom is then said to "define the attributes of personhood."

Those with any knowledge of Jewish or Islamic or Christian

theology will instantly recognize this supposed liberty to define existence, meaning, the universe, and human life as the freedom these theologies ascribe uniquely to their God. It is in fact a freedom of which no one ever dreamed apart from the influence of these theologies. According to the Abrahamic religions, there is indeed one whose personhood is defined by such liberty — and only one.

Jews and Christians and Muslims stipulate the difference between God and what is not God by recognizing a particular mode of freedom in God and denying it to all else; the National Organization for Women and its allies claim explicitly and precisely that freedom for themselves, and the court has now written that claim into our law. What is asserted by "pro-choice" ideologists and the court is straightforwardly a theology, one of an explicitly anti-biblical sort.

The conflict began with Eve and Adam: between the Creator and those of his creatures who fancy themselves for his job, between the God who as Lord of his universe calls and enables us to enter the mysterious liberty and meaning that he himself has and that is for us, and our insistence on a universe and liberty and meaning and mystery that we intend to be for ourselves. The notion of a human "right to define one's own concept of existence" would of course be jejune in any case, whether or not there is the biblical God, but that is not the point here. The "pro-choice" movement is a campaign to carry out Sartre's dictum that even if we knew there were the biblical God, it would be necessary to pretend we did not, in order to be free in the way we think we want to be free.

Euthanasia

Finally, we can hardly ignore the culture clash that is most upcoming and may become the fiercest of them all: the conflict between those who assert and those who deny a right to terminate the lives of persons lacking a certain describable quality of life, sometimes at their request or with their permission and sometimes without it. To what used to be called "mercy killing" we must now add "doctor-assisted suicide" and "withdrawal of treatment," where by "treatment" is meant provision of nourishment, liquid or respiration, so that "withdrawing treatment" means putting to death by starvation, dehydration, or asphyxiation.

The heart of the West's medical ethic has heretofore been the distinction between allowing to die and killing. Those responsible for the sick have been permitted in certain circumstances to do the first and commanded never to do the second. The distinction is sometimes (though not often) difficult to apply, and is easy to attack with sophistically chosen hard cases. Just so it is a perfectly ordinary and intelligible distinction of the kind with which moral reasoning always has to work.

According to the ancient rule, a particular treatment may be refused or withheld if it is useless or unduly burdensome, but any action leading predictably to death may not be undertaken because the sufferer or her caretakers judge her life itself to be useless or unduly burdensome. Thus, for example, medication to alleviate suffering may be continued as needed dosages achieve levels known to be lethal, but may not be leap-frogged to such levels in advance of clinical need.

Why would we want to dispense with this rule? "Compassion" is the invariable answer: "Our child" or "my patient" — or, in the case of assisted suicide, "I" — is said to be "suffering uselessly and intolerably," so that "love" itself demands the killing. But the question is, whose compassion is here responsible? The God of Abraham is the God who "gives life and death," who claims sole responsibility precisely at this point. It indeed is often hard to believe in his compassion — and those who trust in him have seldom claimed it was easy. But where his commands are remembered, prayer, sometimes even for death, is our love's last recourse, and never poison or starvation or strangulation.

It would be too simple to say that having lost cultural reliance on the Lord's compassion we are driven to substitute our own. It is rather the other way around: Having determined to substitute our compassion for his, we are driven to deny him.

It is not by accident that in America's recent history the demand for compassion's right to kill has followed the victory of sheer choice's right to kill. As soon as choice is enthroned as the supreme value of life, it becomes apparent that a life merely so lived is empty; choice must have some content or it is nothing. And the "value" with the least and so most tolerable content is love-as-sentiment. Having tried naked choice as our only meaning, we find that we are not up to such Nietzschean rigor, and fall back a half step on "loving" choice. The defining test of choice is still, necessarily, someone's death.

The horridly clear-sighted Nietzsche saw two death-dealing specters at the nihilist end: the glorious superman and the feeble "last man." In the end we prove incapable of the superman's ghastly courage, and grasp instead the last man's sentimentality, choosing death out of sentiment for our fellows or in self-pity for ourselves. Once this is in place, we will then find some way to understand also unilateral choice to abort as loving choice — and indeed we are already well along with that project.

The last man makes his Adamic move by demanding the right to kill as compassion moves him. Both the superman and the last man, according to Nietzsche, create themselves in revolt against the biblical God.

Another God

I could examine other phenomena of the culture-wars, but would come to no more logical end than this, another question: Is the opposition to Abraham's God united only by a shared aversion, or is there a deity on that side also? Perhaps we can find a preliminary answer simply by going back over the phenomena just discussed, to see if they reveal the lineaments of any known alternative divine claimant.

The God of Abraham is jealous. *Per contra*, if there is some one deity honored by pluralist ideology, its godhead must be its very lack of personal identity or concern. It must be an abstract divinity lurking behind the gods of the many religions and yogas, and therefore capable of being revealed by and as any or all of them. Just so, one can only refer to this god as "it," which is how I have begun and will continue.

The God of Abraham has his own ideas and purposes, with which his creatures must reckon. *Per contra*, a divinity could exist that is desirable precisely for its lack of such defined will, a sheer eternity, available as the screen on which we may project our several ideas and purposes in order to assure ourselves of them.

The God of Abraham is — to introduce just one term of the old theology — *a se.* That is, he is free to begin with himself, and so is free to choose also his world and his creatures and his and their meanings. *Per contra,* there could be a deity whose very function was to support us in our choices, to assuage the burden we assume when we declare ourselves *a se.*

The God of Abraham is love. Which is to say that he is beyond our understanding, for actual love is the one great mystery even when *we* practice it. *Per contra,* a deity could exist by whom the last man excuses himself for not being the superman, an hypostasis not of love but of perfectly understandable "acceptance."

Our civilization's religious history knows indeed a deity defined by these very marks. Moreover, it has always been our chief alternative to the God of Abraham. The noncompetitive "mysteries" of late antiquity knew this deity as the common ground of their several aspirations, and gnostics elaborated its manifestations and secrets. The Enlightenment despised this deity, but could tolerate none other for actual worship and so worshiped not at all or secretly and guiltily, *à la* Immanuel Kant. Romantics and Spinozists overcame the aversion. And if there was a "God that failed," he was yet another, slightly esoteric, avatar of this same divinity. It seems fairly obvious that just this deity is indeed jointly worshiped by the anti-Abrahamic alliance.

Since America decided that her initial teacher, John Calvin, was too forbidding, we have had a special national inclination to late antiquity's mystery-deity. Emerson was its first clear prophet among us, but there have been many since. The nation the Enlightenment made has indeed been a sort of collective and large-writ Kant: We have made space for romantic religiosity by creating a "private" sphere for its guilty enjoyment. Often enough, we have confusedly worshiped late-antique deity even in supposed synagogues and churches; and in these last throes of Christianity's authority among us, the confusion is so deep that gnostic devotees are established as the bureaucratic elite of "mainline" Christian denominations. Our "culture-wars" are but the final stage of a long struggle.

Can peace be declared? Apocalyptic types, among whom I appear on every other day, think not. If it can, there are several possibilities.

The gates of hell will not prevail against the Lord's people — and the Jews have empirical confirmation of this, hell having already made its attempt. But there is no guarantee that the American church or synagogue will endure, and they give every present indication of having lost the will to live. Perhaps a sort of peace will come by a repristinated and (this time) untroubled sway of Western antiquity's late religiosity, in which all gods are worshiped but the jealous one.

Or perhaps Christianity and Judaism, having lost their cultural authority in America, can nerve themselves to a clean break and return to their normal outsider positions. A much reduced and concentrated church and a renewed synagogue might perhaps again live as sometimes licit and sometimes harassed outsider sects, as in the second and early third centuries of our civilization's antiquity — or as in much of the world recently. Perhaps this would not be the peace anyone would choose. But both Christianity and Judaism have been at their creative and faithful best in just such situations.

Most desirable would be, of course, that a genuinely plural culture and state were achieved, so that a smaller church and renewed synagogue could continue to contribute to the larger society. For this to happen, America's public elites would have to recover from pluralist ideology, in order to allow actually plural public life, that is, advocacy and debate of authentic commitments. Our public elites would have to apostasize from their now common deity, opening the way in our society for the presence and voice of Buddhism, Taoism, shamanism, and so forth in their own plural characters, and not as mere ways not to be Christian or Jewish. As to that deity itself, neither church nor synagogue can stop trying to free our fellow humans from its reign of empty freedom and sentiment, that is, of death; and this too would have to be honored. These last possibilities are, of course, for another essay.

Christian Universalism:
The Nonexclusive Particularity
of Salvation in Christ

J. A. DiNoia, O.P.

I s Jesus Christ the unique mediator of salvation? I was one of five panelists assigned to address this question at a recent meeting of Catholic theologians. I was the first to speak and, as it turned out, the only panelist prepared to advance an unqualified affirmative response to the question. Why is this? Why would a group of Catholic theologians decline to affirm what, until recently, would have been considered an unquestionable tenet of ecumenical Christian faith?

As the session unfolded, it became clear that their reluctance to do so was motivated at least in part by a desire to avoid giving offense to religious people of other traditions. The underlying premise of their remarks, and of the ensuing discussion, seemed to be this: To ascribe a uniquely salvific role to Jesus Christ would constitute a denial of the salvific role of other religious founders (like the Buddha and Muhammad) and thus would be an affront to their communities.

The way that many theologians think about this issue has been influenced by the pluralist theology of religions popularized by John Hick, Paul Knitter, and others.[1] Indeed, Paul Knitter was one of the

---

1. Paul Knitter has advanced his position on this issue in a widely read book called *No Other Name? A Critical Survey of Christian Attitudes toward Other Religions* (Maryknoll: Orbis Books, 1985). John Hick has recently restated his position in *An Interpretation of Religion: Human Respondents to the Transcendent*

panelists at the session I mentioned above. In a nutshell, pluralists claim that in one way or another all religions aim at salvation. In John Hick's influential definition, salvation is the movement from self-centeredness to "Reality-centeredness." Since, according to pluralists, ultimate Reality is incomprehensible and ineffable, no one religious description can claim primacy over rival descriptions, and no tradition can claim exclusive rights to the means of salvation.

In the pluralist perspective, therefore, each religious founder must be regarded as in some sense a savior. Exclusive or unique status, with respect to the knowledge of, provision for, or access to, salvation can no more be claimed for Jesus of Nazareth than it can be claimed for Gautama the Buddha or for Muhammad. Naturally, pluralists do not deny that these founders were unique historical personalities. What they deny is that any one of them could provide a uniquely privileged or exclusive access to salvation.

It follows for pluralists that Christian theologians cannot give a simple affirmative answer to the question, Is Jesus Christ the unique mediator of salvation? On the basis of their study of religious traditions, pluralist philosophers and theologians contend that salvation, though diversely mediated, is nonetheless universally accessible. It is not just in order to avoid giving offense to other religious people that pluralists have championed this view. Pluralists argue on empirical and philosophical grounds that a soteriological structure underlies all religious traditions and thus variously orients their adherents to "Reality" as it is diversely figured in these traditions. Only in this way can Christian theologians affirm the universality of salvation and of religious truth, at least as possibilities, without giving offense to other religious people.

To be sure, pluralists are not the only theologians who have been concerned with the salvation of persons who are not Christians. According to the typology prevailing in current theology of religions,

---

(New Haven: Yale Univ. Press, 1989). With Paul Knitter, Hick edited an influential volume of essays, *The Myth of Christian Uniqueness: Toward a Pluralistic Theology of Religions* (Maryknoll: Orbis Books, 1987), in which the pluralist case is pressed from a variety of standpoints. For responses to these essays and to pluralism generally, see Gavin D'Costa, ed., *Christian Uniqueness Reconsidered: The Myth of a Pluralistic Theology of Religions* (Maryknoll: Orbis Books, 1990).

the chief alternative positions on this issue are represented by exclusivism and inclusivism. In contrast to pluralists, both exclusivists and inclusivists would have no difficulty in giving an affirmative answer to the question, Is Jesus Christ the unique mediator of salvation? For all their sharp differences, exclusivists and inclusivists concur in their avowal of the uniquely salvific role of Christ. But exclusivists deny the possibility of salvation for non-Christians who do not before death explicitly profess faith in Christ. Inclusivists, on the other hand, allow for the possibility of salvation chiefly on the grounds of some form of implicit faith in Christ, combined with a morally upright life, on the part of non-Christians.[2]

The Christian concern not to give offense to other religious people is a praiseworthy one, while the concern to allow for the possibility of their salvation is a doctrinally crucial one. But suppose that, far from being an affront to other religious traditions, a strong Christian affirmation of the uniqueness of Christ's salvific role were fundamental to traditional Christian universalism. Suppose, in other words, that the particularity of salvation in Christ were nonexclusive. Suppose, further, that an affirmation of this nonexclusive particularity of salvation in Christ were not an obstacle to but a condition for genuine respect for other religious people.

I have argued this position at length elsewhere.[3] It rests not only on central Christian doctrines but also on the suggestion that "salvation" is not a term that encompasses what all religions seek, but is a properly Christian designation for that which should be sought above all else in life. Salvation has a distinctively Christian content: transformation in Christ with a view to ultimate communion with the triune God. Even where other religious communities employ the term "salvation," their conceptions of the aim of life differ from one another and from that espoused by Christian communities. By framing the agenda of theology of religions primarily

2. For a historical perspective on this debate, see Francis A. Sullivan, *Salvation Outside the Church? Tracing the History of the Catholic Response* (New York: Paulist, 1992). For a reliable survey of the current discussion, though from a largely inclusivist vantage point, see Gavin D'Costa, *Theology and Religious Pluralism* (Oxford: Basil Blackwell, 1986).

3. See J. A. DiNoia, *The Diversity of Religions: A Christian Perspective* (Washington, D.C.: The Catholic University of America Press, 1992).

in terms of the possibility of extra-Christian salvation, pluralists and inclusivists often fail to give enough weight to the specificity and distinctiveness of religious aims. Inclusivists fail to notice their distinctiveness because they tend to reinterpret non-Christian patterns and aims in Christian terms. More at the center of my attention in this essay, however, are pluralists who make salvation an all-encompassing designation for the variety of aims that religious traditions espouse and commend.

If the issues here were framed differently, it might turn out that to affirm Christ's unique role in salvation is not to exclude persons who are not Christians but to embrace them. In other words, it might turn out that we could give a strong affirmative answer to the question, Is Jesus Christ the unique mediator of salvation? and still both show respect for other religious people and include them in the final consummation of all things for which we have reason, only in Christ, to hope.

In order to reframe these issues, and at the same time to identify what seems to be the weakness especially of typical pluralist approaches to them, I want to engage in an experiment. I will compare the question, Is Jesus Christ the unique mediator of salvation? with the question, Is the Buddha the unique revealer of the Dharma?

Suppose that I pose this second question to a Buddhist friend. Along with most other Buddhists, she will answer it affirmatively. The Dharma comprises all that concerns Nirvana and its attainment. Even though Buddhists commonly insist that knowledge of the Dharma is in principle accessible to anyone, still they regard Gautama's discovery and teaching of the Dharma as unique in this era.[4]

Consider how the conversation might proceed at this point. If my Buddhist friend should caution me that I will never attain Nirvana by following the course of life laid out for me by the Christian community, I do not feel anxious about this. I have not been persuaded that seeking Nirvana is what I should be doing. If I did begin to be persuaded of this, then I should undertake to

---

4. See, e.g., the discussion of the uniqueness of the Buddha's discovery and teaching of the Dharma in Sangharakshita, *A Survey of Buddhism*, 5th ed. (Boulder, Colo.: Shambhala Publications, 1980), pp. 37-38.

discover the path and try to make my way along it. I would, in other words, have begun to be a follower of the Buddha. I might then even join a Buddhist community, or at least become an inquirer. Some Catholics I know have done this very thing. But if I continue to be convinced that it is salvation that I should be seeking and that Christ is the unique mediator of this salvation, then I would continue on the Christian path.

One thing to notice about this hypothetical encounter between me and my Buddhist friend is that I have not felt affronted by her warning that I shall not attain Nirvana unless I follow the Excellent Eightfold Path taught uniquely by the Buddha. On the contrary, my initial reaction is that what she has said to me makes perfect sense. If the Excellent Eightfold Path is the way to Nirvana, and if I do not choose to pursue this path, then it follows that I may not reach Nirvana. But, since I have as yet no desire to attain and enjoy Nirvana, I am not offended by this reasoning. I have not been persuaded that Nirvana is what I should be seeking.

Without trying to field a "definition" of religion — something that has proven notoriously difficult to do — I could say that the Christian community and the Buddhist community (with their various subcommunities) both seem to have some conception of an ultimate aim of life and have developed a pattern of life geared toward attaining it. Other major religious communities share this tendency as well.[5] What is ultimate, whether it be a transcendent agent or as yet unrealized state of being, invades life at every moment, and summons the community's members to order and shape their lives in view of this aim. The world's religious communities differ in their descriptions of the aims that are ultimate in this sense (e.g., the extinction of the self or communion with the triune God) as well as in their provision for the cultivation of patterns of life ordered to the attainment and enjoyment of such aims (e.g., the Dharma or the gospel). But they seem to agree in espousing and

5. In his *Doctrines of Religious Communities* (New Haven: Yale Univ. Press, 1987), William A. Christian, Sr., has observed: "There seems to be a deep-seated tendency in the major religious communities to develop a comprehensive pattern of life . . . which bears on all human interests . . . and on all situations in which human beings find themselves" (p. 186).

commending comprehensive aims of life, and in striving to shape the lives of their members with a view to those aims.

I can now formulate a preliminary result of the consideration of the hypothetical conversation between me and my Buddhist friend. If the assertion "The Buddha is the unique revealer of the Dharma" is not offensive to me, then why should the assertion "Jesus Christ is the unique mediator of salvation" be offensive to Buddhists, or, for that matter, to Muslims, Vedantists, or Jews? A Jewish rabbi once said to me, revealingly: "Jesus Christ is the answer to a question I have never asked." This remark suggests that we might be on the right track in our reflections. Salvation in the Christian sense, it implies, is not what the rabbi is seeking. Asking the question to which Jesus Christ is the answer commits oneself to an inquiry (logically speaking) that may lead to the adoption of a Christian way of life. At least in part, this will mean that what Christians aim for, as expressed by the umbrella term "salvation," has begun to look appealing or even ultimately important. One might conclude: *This* is what I should be aiming for in my life. But what would this be?

When Christians try to answer this question, we find ourselves becoming quite specific. When we try to say what comprises salvation, we find ourselves talking about the triune God; the incarnation, passion, death, and resurrection of Jesus Christ; grace, sin, and justification; transfiguration and divinization; faith, hope, and charity; the commandments and the moral virtues; and many other characteristically Christian things as well. We should not be surprised if, in trying to answer a cognate question, a member of another religious community, say a Buddhist, should also become very specific about Nirvana and all that bears on its attainment. We should not be surprised, furthermore, if the descriptions of salvation and Nirvana do not coincide. But, for the moment, let us continue the experiment by sketching some of the things that a Christian description of salvation might have to include.

Allowing for variations across its various subcommunities, we can understand the ecumenical Christian community to teach that the ultimate aim of life is a communion of life — a communion of life with the Father, through the Son, and in the Holy Spirit. According to ecumenical Christian faith, this is a truth proclaimed by

Christ and a destiny made possible for us by his passion, death, and resurrection. This is what Christians mean by salvation: The term embraces both the goal of ultimate communion and the empowerment to attain and enjoy it.

Human persons are called to nothing less than communion with the Father, Son, and Holy Spirit, and with each other in them. Indeed, Christianity affirms that the triune God could not bring about a more intimate union with created persons than that which has already been initiated in baptism and will be fulfilled for us in Christ. Ultimate communion involves nothing less than becoming part of the trinitarian family. The principle and agent of this communion for us is Christ. Just as Christ is Son by nature — a member of the divine family of the Trinity in virtue of his being the Son of the Father — so human persons are to be sons and daughters by adoption. Our fellowship with Christ and with each other in him brings us into the divine trinitarian family.

But if we are destined to enjoy this ultimate communion, then we must change. We must become fit for it. Interpersonal communion with God is only "natural" to uncreated persons; for created persons, who are also sinners, such communion is possible only through justification and grace. Through the redeeming grace of Christ and, specifically, through the transformation that this grace makes possible, we are rendered "fit" participants in the communion of the Father, Son, and Holy Spirit. Our transformation will be a conformation: The more we become like Christ, the more surely do we discover our true selves, the unique persons created by the triune God to share in the divine life and to enjoy the personal life of the Trinity. As Catholics pray in one of the Sunday prefaces: "Father, . . . [y]ou sent him as one like ourselves, though free from sin, that you might see and love in us what you see and love in him."[6]

However, this conformation does not amount to a mere conformity. The conformation to Christ that is the principle of our transformation is not a mere cloning but the realization of our distinctive and unique personal identities. This must be so, for

6. Sundays in Ordinary Time, Preface VII, *The Sacramentary* (New York: Catholic Book Publishing Co., 1974), p. 443.

otherwise the communion to which this transformation is directed could not be consummated. The image of God in us consists precisely in the spiritual capacities for knowing and loving that make interpersonal communion possible. But authentic interpersonal communion presupposes the full realization of the individual persons who enter into it. Thus, if Christ is to be the principle and pattern of our transformation, in being conformed to him we must each discover and realize our own unique identities as persons, and be healed of the sinful dispositions that obstruct the flourishing of our true selves.

This is the force of the astonishing saying of Christ:

> If a man wants to be my disciple, let him deny himself and take up his cross and follow me. For whoever wants to save his life will lose it, and whoever loses his life for my sake will find it. For what will it profit a man if he gains the whole world but loses his life? Or what will he give in return for his life? (Matt. 16:24-26)

None of us, whether as teachers, parents, or pastors — no matter how inflated our conceptions of ourselves or how confident our sense of our abilities — would ever dare to say to anybody in our charge that they will find their true selves by imitating us. In effect, Christ asserts that an indefinite number of human persons will find their distinctive identities by being conformed to Christ. A moment's reflection shows us that only the Son of God could make such an assertion. No mere human could do so. Only the inexhaustibly rich, perfect Image of God who is the person of the Son in human nature could constitute the principle and pattern for the transformation and fulfillment of every human person who has ever lived.

When Christians affirm that Jesus Christ is the unique mediator of salvation, something like the above can stand as a summary of what they mean. Leave aside for a moment the question whether such a description includes or excludes persons who are not Christians. What we need to consider first, as we continue to reflect on my hypothetical conversation with a Buddhist friend, is whether such a description of what Christians mean by salvation is offensive to persons who are not Christians — Buddhists, for example. Informed of what a Christian means by salvation, would there be reason for a Buddhist to feel excluded by the assertion that Jesus Christ is the unique mediator of salvation?

We have seen that salvation has a specific content for Christians: It entails an interpersonal communion, made possible by Christ, between human persons and the Father, Son, and Holy Spirit. At least at first sight, this seems to be something very different from what Buddhists can be supposed to be seeking when they follow the Excellent Eightfold Path that leads them on the way to realizing enlightenment and the extinction of self in Nirvana.[7] At least on the face of things, what Buddhists mean by "Nirvana" and what Christians mean by "salvation" do not seem to coincide. This does not mean that they are opposed; it remains to be seen whether seeking salvation and seeking Nirvana are complementary to each other or related in some as yet unspecified manner.[8] However, it seems clear that interpersonal communion is a very different thing from the extinction of the self entailed in Nirvana. Many forms of Buddhism are concerned to cultivate dispositions that increasingly unmask the illusoriness of personal identity. As I noted above in my sketch of what most Christians mean by salvation, Christians understand personal identity to be of permanent, indeed eternal, significance because eternity centrally involves interpersonal communion.

Let us return to my hypothetical conversation with a Buddhist friend. You will recall that we left the conversation at the point when she cautioned me that I would not reach Nirvana unless I

7. The statement of my argument here is deliberately hypothetical. My purpose is not to present an account of Buddhism, though I have striven to be accurate about Buddhist doctrines. Rather, it is to render plausible the claim, fundamental to my argument, that "Nirvana" and "salvation" seem to designate significantly different aims of life, and thus call forth distinctive patterns of life in the members of Buddhist and Christian communities respectively, and to render implausible the pluralist claim that salvation encompasses what Christians mean by ultimate communion with the triune God and what Buddhists (seem to) mean by Nirvana.

8. For a philosophical analysis of religious disagreements, see William A. Christian, Sr., *Oppositions of Religious Doctrines* (New York: Seabury, 1972). For a discussion of the kinds of arguments that such disagreements might give rise to in interreligious dialogue, see Paul J. Griffiths, *An Apology for Apologetics: A Study in the Logic of Interreligious Dialogue* (Maryknoll: Orbis Books, 1991).

followed the Excellent Eightfold Path. This warning was not disturbing to me, for I do not want to attain Nirvana. Suppose that when the conversation resumes I offer a description of what Christians mean by salvation, a description not unlike the one presented above. Would we be surprised to find that my Buddhist friend wants no part of this? It is difficult for us to understand and accept that what we regard as most important — more so than anything else, absolutely speaking — other religious people challenge or repudiate. Buddhist communities in all their variety possess highly ramified teachings about the true aim of life and about the means to attain it. These teachings do not, at least on the surface, coincide with what Christians teach about these very matters. Buddhists do not want ultimate communion; they do not seek it, and, insofar as they think about it, they may regard us as misguided for wanting and seeking it. For, by wanting and seeking ultimate communion we remain, from a Buddhist point of view, incorrigibly attached to the very conceptions of personal identity that constitute the chief obstacle on the way to Nirvana.

Gautama the Buddha is the authority on these matters. He discovered and taught the Dharma, and through it attained enlightenment. His role in revealing the Dharma to others is regarded by most of his followers as something original, at least in the present epoch. Hence, while it makes good sense for Buddhists to affirm that the Buddha is the unique revealer of the Dharma, it makes little sense for them to be offended when Christians describe Jesus Christ as the unique mediator of salvation. Buddhists regard Christian beliefs about this as misguided and perhaps only partially true, but they will not be anxious or offended by such a Christian affirmation. They are not interested in seeking and attaining salvation as Christians understand it.

To be sure, some people — pluralists in particular — want to define "salvation" so broadly that it includes both what Christians mean by it and what Buddhists mean by Nirvana. On this account of things, my hypothetical encounter with a Buddhist friend would not present either of us with a choice between seeking Nirvana and seeking salvation. Some would say that to think that there is a serious choice here is, religiously speaking, overly literalistic and even simpleminded. Indeed, pluralists contend, precisely at this juncture the superiority of pluralist theology of religions is displayed. Pluralists argue that all religious communities advance their members toward specific aims — communion or enlightenment, as the case may be — that are surpassed or transcended by a more ultimate, but indescribable, aim. All religious communities seek this yet more ultimate aim with varying degrees of clarity and success. Not only is this conception closer to the truth of the matter, it also provides the basis for the sympathetic understanding, fruitful dialogue, and mutual respect that are desperately needed today.

In fact, however, this basic premise of pluralist theology of religions will not stand up under close scrutiny. Even if religious communities were prepared to accept some such description of what they are about — something few of them show any inclination to do — it still remains true that they espouse and commend specific aims that differ from one another. Furthermore, these specific aims call forth distinctive patterns of life in each of the major religious traditions and in local traditions as well. Certain kinds of life are understood to foster the enjoyment of certain kinds of ends of life, and others to obstruct this enjoyment. This seems to be an ineradicable feature of the characteristic discourse and ethos of most religious communities. Individual lives come to be shaped by the ultimate aims that are sought. So even if the true aim of life were one that transcended the particular aims of all religious traditions — something stipulated by pluralists — no one could seek it. No one could undertake to order life in such a way as to attain and enjoy an ultimate aim of life of which no description could be given.

But this goes directly against the grain of characteristic religious affirmation and conviction. Religious people, by and large, believe themselves to be in possession of understandings, incomplete though they may be, of what is ultimately important in life and how to orient life in its direction. Significant disagreements obtain among the major and local religious traditions about these matters. Pluralist theology of religions does not so much explain these disagreements as explain them away. In this way, pluralism seems to offer a massive redescription, rather than an interpretation, of religious beliefs and practices, and of the arresting differences among them.

Thus the following statements are not problematic in the way that many people, like those I joined on the theological panel, seem to think: "Jesus Christ is the unique mediator of salvation" and "The Buddha is the unique revealer of the Dharma." Were representatives of Christian or Buddhist communities to retreat from advancing such claims, it is not clear what they would have to offer to the world. There would be no compelling, or even interesting, reasons to persevere in membership in these communities, or indeed to seek it.

The great challenge facing present-day Christian theology of religions and interreligious conversation is to avoid minimizing the distinctive features of the major religious traditions through a well-intentioned universalism. Christian confidence in the universal scope of salvation rests on convictions about the historical career and perduring agency of Jesus Christ. Only if his identity is affirmed in its fullness — in accord with the holy Scripture, the great councils, and the church's liturgy — as the Son of God who became man and died for us, can the hope of Christians for themselves and for others be sustained. "For in him all the fullness of God was pleased to dwell, and through him God was pleased to reconcile all things, whether on earth or in heaven, by making peace through the blood of his cross" (Col. 1:19-20).

If the salvation that the triune God wills for the entire human race entails ultimate communion with the three persons, then the creaturely and sinful obstacles to this communion must be overcome. It has never been claimed that anyone but Jesus Christ could overcome these obstacles. Through him we are both healed and raised to an adoptive participation in the life of the Trinity. The obstacles to this participation are either overcome or not. If they are not overcome, then Christians have nothing for which to hope, for themselves or for others. In that case, they will hawk an empty universalism on the highways of the world. When Christians abandon the proclamation of Christ's unique mediatorship, they have no other mediatorship with which to replace it. How persons who are not now explicit believers in Christ are to share in the salvation he alone makes possible is a large topic that I have not addressed in this paper. But if Christians no longer confess Christ's unique mediatorship in making ultimate communion a real possibility for created persons, then the problem of how non-Christians can share in it is not resolved. It simply evaporates. True Christian universalism depends on the affirmation of the nonexclusive particularity of salvation in Jesus Christ.

Serving the One True God

Robert L. Wilken

One of the lessons read at the Easter Vigil is the story of Shadrach, Meshach, and Abednego in the fiery furnace. It is a good story told well and not without irony. Each year when it is read I can hardly conceal a smile as the author lists (and not just once), the titles of the king's advisors — the satraps, prefects, governors, counselors, treasurers, justices, magistrates, and officials of the provinces — or takes delight (again not just once) in naming the musical instruments that called people to worship the golden statue — the sound of the horn, pipe, lyre, trigon, harp, drum, and the entire musical ensemble. This year, however, it was another section of the lesson that caught my attention. After the deliverance of Shadrach, Meshach, and Abednego from the fiery furnace, King Nebuchadnezzar says, "Blessed be the God of Shadrach, Meshach, and Abednego. . . . They disobeyed the king's command and yielded up their bodies rather than serve and worship any god except their own God" (Dan. 3:28).

It is a sign of the times that on the holiest night of the year the phrase from Daniel "serve and worship any god except their own God" leaped out at me. In the past I remember listening intently to the reading of Genesis 1, to the account of the Passover, or the exhortations of Deuteronomy to the newly baptized. But this Easter the words of King Nebuchadnezzar brought to mind the first commandment: You shall have no other gods besides me. In the waning years of the twentieth century the time

49

has come for Christians to bear witness to the worship of the one true God.

Practical atheism (that is, secularism) has undermined beliefs, attitudes, and conventions that have nurtured our civilization for centuries. Within the space of a few decades patterns of life that former ages took for granted have been undermined by haughty and self-righteous critics. The changes that we are witnessing are not the inevitable alterations by which older ways adapt to new circumstances. They are the result of a systematic dismembering, a "trashing" of our culture that is "intentional, not accidental," as Myron Magnet writes in his recent *The Dream and the Nightmare*.[1] Nothing is left untouched, whether it be our most cherished institutions, the roles that have defined one's place in family, neighborhood, and city, or assumptions about duty, love, virtue, honor, and modesty. All are subject to the scalpel of impatient reformers; what has been received from our parents and grandparents and from their parents and grandparents must submit to our unforgiving formulas for correction.

The goal, of course, is to dismantle the common culture, to make everything into a subculture. Secularism wants religious practice, especially Christian practice, banished to a private world of feelings and attitudes, at the same time that it expands the realm of the public to include every aspect of life. The earlier secularist appearance of tolerance toward religion is now seen to have been a sham. Nor does secularism sustain any sense of obligation to the past. The texture of memory that is essential to a common culture cannot be kept intact if the past is not lovingly transmitted to those who come after — even should some of its monuments offend us.

Christianity has proved to be more tolerant than are the current revisionists. Christian culture, as Rémi Brague, the French philosopher, observed, has "resisted the temptation to absorb in itself what it had inherited from either the Greeks or the Jews — to suck in the content and to throw away the empty husk."[2] Over its long history the Christian tradition has cultivated a studied open-

---

1. Myron Magnet, *The Dream and the Nightmare* (New York: W. Morrow, 1993), p. 196.
2. Rémi Brague, "Christ, Culture and the New Europe," *First Things* (August/September 1992): 40.

ness to the wisdom of former ages, even when it offered intellectual resources to challenge Christian faith. Recall how the *philosophes* depended on the inheritance of Greek antiquity in their attacks on Christianity. Yet for centuries Christian institutions have nurtured the study of the classics. Christianity is an essential ingredient in our culture, says Braque, for its form "enables it to remain open to whatever can come from the outside and enrich the hoard of its experiences with the human and divine."[3]

The ferocity of the current assault on the legacy of Christian culture has, however, brought a clarity of vision. The alternatives are set before us with unusual starkness: Either there will be a genuine renewal of Christian culture — there is no serious alternative — or we will be enveloped by the darkness of paganism in which the worship of the true God is abandoned and forgotten. The sources of the cultural crisis, it turns out, are theological.

In his lectures on Christianity and culture T. S. Eliot posed the issue of Christianity and Western culture in terms that were remarkably prescient.[4] Writing in 1939 on the eve of World War II, Eliot said that the "choice before us is between the formation of a new Christian culure, and the acceptance of a pagan one." Distinguishing three epochs in the history of Christianity and Western culture, he spoke of the period when Christianity was a "minority in a society of positive pagan traditions," a second period when the society as a whole — law, education, literature, art, as well as religion — was formed by Christianity, and a third, our own period, in which the culture has become "mainly negative, but which, so far as it is positive, is still Christian." In his view "a society has not ceased to be Christian until it has become something else." Yet, he continued, "I do not think that [a culture] can remain negative," and it is conceivable that an attempt will be made to build a new culture on wholly different "spiritual" foundations. Eliot's proposal is that the way to meet this challenge is to form a "new Christian culture."[5]

Eliot's lectures are filled with much wisdom. He said that

3. Ibid.

4. T. S. Eliot, *Christianity and Culture: The Idea of a Christian Society and Notes towards the Definition of Culture* (New York: Harcourt Brace Jovanovich, 1977).

5. Ibid., pp. 9-10.

"Christianity is communal before being individual,"[6] and that there can be no Christian society where there is no respect for the religious life. "I cannot conceive a Christian society without religious orders, even purely contemplative orders, even enclosed orders."[7] If we are to speak of a Christian society, says Eliot, we "must treat Christianity with a great deal more intellectual respect than is our wont." And we must be concerned to make clear "its difference from the kind of society in which we are now living." Above all is his observation that touches more directly on theology: It is, he writes, a "very dangerous inversion" for Christian thinkers "to advocate Christianity, not because it is true, but because it might be beneficial." Instead of showing that Christianity "provides a foundation for morality," one must show "the necessity of Christian morality from the truth of Christianity." "It is not enthusiasm, but dogma, that differentiates a Christian from a pagan society."[8]

Dogma and truth are not the kind of words that will pass the test of political correctness, yet — or perhaps therefore — they are useful in helping us precisely to identify the distinctively theological task that lies before us. It is time to return to first principles, to the first commandment, and to take up anew the challenge faced by Christians many centuries ago when the Christian movement was first making its way in the Roman Empire. Christians are now called to persuade others (including many within the churches) that our first duty as human beings is to honor and venerate the one true God, and that without God society disintegrates into an aggregate of self-centered and competing interests destructive of the commonweal. To meet that challenge Christians must learn again to speak forthrightly about who we are and what we know of God.

The Christian faith, as Eliot reminds us, is concerned not simply with values or attitudes or feelings or even "beliefs" (in the weak sense that we use the term today), but with truth. Christianity is based not simply on experience, tradition, inherited wisdom, and reason, but on God's self-disclosure in history. To be sure, Christian truth has been tested by experience; it has been handed on through a learned tradition in which it has been formulated, criticized,

6. Ibid., p. 47.
7. Ibid., p. 48.
8. Ibid., p. 47.

analyzed, refined, and tested. Thus it has been the bearer of wisdom about what is good in human life, about sexuality, about youthfulness and aging, about work and money, children and family, duty and sacrifice, friendship and love, art, literature, and music. But, as Origen said in responding to Celsus' charges against Christianity, the Christian religion has its origin in "God's manifestation not in human sagacity,"[9] in the appearance of the divine Logos in human form. Christian faith is grounded in what was made known in Christ and confirmed by the Spirit's witness in the church. Consequently Christian thinking, whether about God, Christ, the moral life, or culture, must always begin with what has been revealed.

A pernicious feature of Christian discourse in our day is its tentativeness, the corrosive assumption that everything we teach and practice is to be subject to correction by appeals to putative evidence, whether from science, history, or the religious experience of others. Nicholas Wolterstorff and Alvin Plantinga call this the evidentialist fallacy, the claim that it is not rational for a person to be a Christian unless one "holds his religious convictions on the basis of other beliefs of his which give to those convictions adequate evidential support."[10] In this view one's religious beliefs are to be held "probable" until evidence is deployed from elsewhere to support and legitimate them. The "presumption of atheism" must be the starting point of all our thinking, even about God.

One way of responding to this line of criticism has been to offer arguments for the existence of God based on what is considered evidence acceptable to any reasonable person. Conventional wisdom had it that proof of the existence of God has to be established without reference to the specifics of Christianity (or Judaism) or to the experience of the church. Atheism is to be countered by a defense of theism, not of Christian revelation. But this strategy has failed, and in his book *At the Origins of Modern Atheism* Michael Buckley has helped us to understand why.[11] To

9. Origen, *Contra Celsum* 3.14, trans. Henry Chadwick (Cambridge: Harvard Univ. Press, 1965), p. 137.

10. Alvin Plantinga and Nicholas Wolterstorff, eds., *Faith and Rationality: Reason and Belief in God* (Notre Dame: Univ. of Notre Dame Press, 1983), p. 6.

11. Michael J. Buckley, S.J., *At the Origins of Modern Atheism* (New Haven: Yale Univ. Press, 1987).

defend the existence of God, Christian thinkers in early modern times excluded all appeals to Christian behavior or practices, the very things that give Christianity its power and have been its most compelling testimony to the reality of God. Arguments against atheism inevitably took the form of arguments from nature or design, without reference to Christ, to the sacraments, to the practice of prayer, or to the church. Buckley's book is an account of how this came to be, but within its historical description is an implicit argument that the "god defined in religion cannot be affirmed or supported adequately . . . without the unique reality that is religion."[12] Or, to put the matter more concretely: "What god is, and even that god is, has its primordial evidence in the person and in the event that is Jesus Christ."[13]

What has given Christianity its strength as a religion, as a way of life, and as an intellectual tradition is that it has always been confident of what it knows. It insisted from the very beginning, again to cite Origen of Alexandria, that the "gospel has a proof which is peculiar to itself."[14] This phrase occurs at the very beginning of Origen's defense of Christianity, *Contra Celsum*. Celsus, a second-century Greek philosopher, had said that the "teaching" that was the source of Christianity was "originally barbarian." By this he meant that Christianity had its origins in Judaism. Origen grants the point and even compliments Celsus that he does not reproach the gospel because it arose among non-Greeks. Yet Celsus adds a condition. He is willing to accept what Christians have received from barbarians as long as Christians are willing to subject their teaching to "Greek proof," that is, to measure it by Celsus' standards as to what is reasonable. Celsus believed that "the Greeks are better able to judge the value of what the barbarians have discovered, and to establish the doctrines and put them into practice by virtue." This is presumptuous, said Origen, for it implies that the "truth of Christianity" is to be decided by a criterion external to itself. Rather, we must say that the "gospel has a *proof* which is *peculiar to itself* and which is more divine than a Greek proof based on dialectical arguments." This more

12. Ibid., p. 362.
13. Ibid., p. 361.
14. Origen, *Contra Celsum* 1.2 (Chadwick, p. 8).

"divine demonstration" is what St. Paul calls the "demonstration of the Spirit and of power" (1 Cor. 2:4).

Insisting that the gospel has a "proof peculiar to itself" did not mean that Christian thinking ignored the claims of reason, dismissing questions that arose from history or experience or logic. In discussions with Greeks, Christian thinkers presented the new faith not only by reference to the Scriptures but also by appeal to classical literature and conceptions, "common ideas" that they shared with other educated men and women. Critics tried to brand the Christians as "fideists," but the charge rang hollow. From the beginning Christians heeded the claims of reason, and it did not take long for their adversaries to learn that they were able to match their opponents argument for argument. Pagan thinkers had no franchise on rationality. Indeed the existence of a serious dialogue between Christians and Greek and Roman philosophers, conducted at the highest intellectual level from the mid-second century to the mid-fifth century, is evidence that Christian thinkers did not supplant reason by faith and authority.[15] The assertion that the gospel had a "proof peculiar to itself" was not a confession of faith but an argument that commended itself to reasonable men and women.

At issue in the argument was the starting point of reason. Origen argued that with the coming of Christ reason had to attend to something new in human experience. In the earliest period of the church's history Christian thinkers did not become philosophers to engage the philosophers. Or, to put the matter more accurately, they did not assume a traditional philosophical starting point to engage in philosophical discussion. In the philosophical texts of the time knowledge of God was derived by certain well-defined ways of knowing, either by a process of successive abstractions (e.g., in the way one one moves from a surface to a line and finally to a point in geometry), by analogy (i.e., by comparing the light of the sun and visible things with the light of God and intellectual things), or by contemplating physical objects and gradually moving to the contemplation of intellectual matters.[16] Against the intellectualism

15. On this point see Robert L. Wilken, *The Christians as the Romans Saw Them* (New Haven: Yale Univ. Press, 1984).

16. See *The Platonic Doctrines of Albinus,* trans. Jeremiah Reedy (Grand Rapids: Phanes Press, 1991), chap. 10, pp. 38-41.

of these ways of knowing God, Christian thinkers argued that the knowledge of God rested on "divine action" and on "God's appearance" among human beings in the person of Christ. Even when speaking to the outsider, they insisted that it was more reasonable to begin with the history of Jesus (and of Israel) than with abstract reasoning. Reason had to begin with what was given. It could no longer be exercised independently of what had taken place in history and what had come to be because of that history, the new reality of the church, a people devoted to the worship of the one true God.

One can see how this conviction worked itself out in Christian thinking in one writer after another, whether in Athanasius' response to the Arians, or in Augustine's efforts to disentangle himself from the sophistries of the Manichees. But Origen is the most illuminating of these because he stands at the beginning of the Christian intellectual tradition. He was the first truly deep thinker to give a firm epistemological foundation to the claim that Christians had come to know God in the person of Christ.

One of the most familiar citations of Plato in this period is a passage from the *Timaeus:* "It is difficult to discover the Father and Maker of this universe; and having found Him, it is impossible to declare Him to all."[17] This text was understood to mean that God was beyond our comprehension, though by the activity of enlightened minds it was possible to have some knowledge of God. Celsus had cited this passage from Plato in his argument against Christians. Origen, in responding to Celsus, said that although Plato's statement was "noble and impressive," it rested on philosophical agnosticism. The best evidence of its limitations was that on the basis of such knowledge of God the philosophers had changed neither their lives nor their manner of worship. Even while claiming to know the true God they went on worshiping the many gods of Greece and Rome — and went on defending such piety as well. For Origen, as well as for Augustine and other critics of the religion of the philosophers, this was the central point. Because their knowledge of God was limited to what they could know by the activity of the mind, they never came to a genuine knowledge

17. Plato, *Timaeus* 28c.

of God. They kept falling back into idolatry. Had Plato known the true God, writes Origen, he "would not have reverenced anything else and called it God and worshipped it, either abandoning the true God or combining with the majesty of God things which ought not to be associated with Him."[18]

The philosophers would not acknowledge that by "becoming flesh" the divine Logos made it possible for human beings to know God more fully than they could by means of human reasoning alone. "We affirm," writes Origen, "that human nature is not sufficient in any way to seek for God and to find Him in his pure nature, unless it is helped by the God who is the object of the search." The knowledge of God is unlike other forms of knowledge, for it begins with God, not with human reasoning. How we conceive of God is dependent on the nature of the reality that is presented to us, that which, in the language of the Bible, is *seen*. The church fathers relied heavily on the Gospel of John in their "epistemology," and especially on John's conjunction between "seeing" and "knowing." Perhaps the most cited text is John 1:18: "No one has ever *seen* God; the only Son, who is in the bosom of the Father, he has made him *known*" (RSV; italics mine).

One sign of the impoverishment of Christian speech in our day is that the term "faith" has been emptied of its cognitive dimensions. As von Balthasar recognized, the logic of Christian discourse has collapsed at this point. "Nothing expresses more unequivocally the profound failure of [theologies that separate the Christ of faith and the Jesus of history] than their deeply anguished, joyless and cheerless tone: torn between knowing and believing, they are no longer able to *see* anything, nor can they be convincing in any visible way." In that connection he appeals to the now classic essay of Pierre Rousselot, "The Eyes of Faith," in support of his point. Rousselot's significance is that he used the term "eyes," hearkening back to the early church fathers and the Bible. The term "eyes . . . indicates that there is something there for faith to see and, indeed, that Christian faith essentially consists in an ability to see what God chooses to show and which cannot be seen without faith."[19]

18. Origen, *Contra Celsum* 7.42 (Chadwick, p. 430).
19. Hans Urs von Balthasar, *The Glory of the Lord* (San Francisco: Ignatius,

The key point here is that faith is not a form of interpretation, one perspective among others, but a seeing of what there is to see, hence a form of knowing. Recall the opening words of the First Epistle of John:

We declare to you what was from the beginning, what we have heard, what we have seen with our eyes, what we have looked at and touched with our hands, concerning the word of life — this life was revealed, and we have seen it and testify to it, and declare to you the eternal life that was with the Father and was revealed to us. (Vv. 1-2)

First John states the primal truth that Christian faith rests on witness, hence the honored place of the martyrs (witnesses) in Christian memory. Yet the witness that is passed on of what was "seen" is never a testimony simply of what has happened in the past. In his *Commentary on I John* St. Augustine noted a curious feature of its opening words. For John does not simply say that he is bearing witness to what he has seen and touched; he says that he is also bearing witness to the "word of life." It does not escape Augustine that the phrase "word of life" does not refer to the body of Christ, which could be seen and handled.

The life itself has been manifested in flesh — that what can be seen by the heart alone might be seen also by the eyes for the healing of hearts. Only by the heart is the Word seen; flesh is seen by the bodily eyes. We had the means of seeing the flesh, but not of seeing the Word: the Word was made flesh which we could see, that the heart, by which we should see the Word, might be healed.[20]

1982), 1:174-75. Pierre Rousselot's essay is now available in English: *The Eyes of Faith,* trans. J. Donceel (New York: Fordham Univ. Press, 1990). For the intellectual context of Rousselot's work see Roger Aubert, *Le Problème de l'Acte de Foi* (Louvain: 1950).

20. Augustine, *Tractatus in Epistolam Johannis* 1.1 (ET in *Augustine: Later Works,* ed. John Burnaby [Philadelphia: 1955], p. 260).

The testimony the church bears from one generation to another is at once a seeing of what was seen and a seeing of what cannot be seen. It is a seeing of what was seen in that the testimony is about something that happened in space and time, something that could be seen with the eyes and touched with the hands, and is part of events that preceded and followed. It is also a seeing of what cannot be seen, in John's terms a "knowing," in that God who cannot be seen is revealed in the events. The testimony that 1 John brings is not simply a witness to a historical event, as one might, for example, tell others about a parade that passed in front of one's house. For that which one "saw" was the "word of life," not simply the words and actions of Jesus of Nazareth.

Faith, then, is not something that is added to knowing; it is constitutive of the act of knowing God. Origen grasped this point with characteristic profundity. In his commentary on John 2:22 ("After he was raised from the dead, his disciples remembered that he had said this; and they *believed* the scripture and the word that Jesus had spoken") Origen cites the words spoken to Thomas in chapter 20, "Blessed are those who have not seen and yet have come to believe." Then he asks: How could it be that those who have not seen and have believed are more blessed than those who have seen and believed? If that is the case, those who come after the apostles will be more blessed than the apostles. But other texts suggest something different, such as "Blessed are your eyes, for they see, and your ears, for they hear" (Matt. 13:16). Simeon said, "Master, now you are dismissing your servant in peace . . . for my eyes have seen your salvation" (Luke 2:29-30). Origen's answer is that in this life faith is imperfect; only at the time of the resurrection will it be complete. But faith will still be *necessary.* Hence it is possible to say of faith what Paul says of knowledge, "now we believe in part." When the "perfection of faith comes," that which is partial will disappear, "for faith complemented by vision is far superior to faith through a mirror."[21]

Faith's certainty comes from participating in the reality that

---

21. Origen, *Commentary on John 10.304-306* (ET in Ronald Heine, *Origen: Commentary on the Gospel According to John Books 1–10* [Washington, D.C.: 1989], pp. 323-24).

is believed, that is, through fellowship with God. "By faith," writes St. Augustine, "we see and we know. For if faith does not yet see, why are we called *illuminati?*"[22] It is not possible to know God from a distance, to be a spectator. Commenting on John 8:19 ("You know neither me nor my Father. If you knew me, you would know my Father also"), Origen explains how the term "know" is used in John and in the Bible as a whole.

> One should take note that the Scripture says that those who are united to something or participate in something are said to *know* that to which they are united or in which they participate. Before such union and fellowship, even if they understand the reasons given for something, they do not know it.

As illustration he mentions the union between Adam and Eve, which the Bible describes as "Adam knew his wife Eve," and union with a prostitute (1 Cor. 6:16-17). This shows, he says, that "knowing" means "being joined to" or "united with."[23] The knowledge of God, then, is experiential. No doubt this is one reason why the knowledge of God is always conjoined with the love of God in early Christian literature. Love implies close familiarity, intimacy, union.

In terms such as these early Christian thinkers defended the worship of the one God. The boldness of the intellectuals as well as the courage of the martyrs (in some cases, e.g., Justin Martyr or Origen, they were the same person) rested on the certainty that comes from "seeing." In a sermon on Acts 1, John Chrysostom said, referring to the phrase "witness of the resurrection," that the apostles, who were witness of the resurrection, did not say: "Angels said this to me, but we have *seen* it."[24] That is the inescapable foundation of Christian belief in God. Matthew Arnold once said: "The uppermost idea with Hellenism is to see things as they really are." That puts things succinctly and backward. Early Christian thinkers insisted that the Greeks *did not* see things as they are. They only saw what lay on the surface. Like the pathetic creatures in Plato's cave,

---

22. Augustine, *Tract. in I Johan.* 4.8.
23. Origen, *Comm. on John 19.4.21-25.*
24. John Chrysostom, *PG* 60.38a.

they saw only shadows and images, not things as they are. For this reason the Greeks had to be corrected, not the Christians. And on this basis Christian thinkers mounted an offensive against the pretensions of their culture. By ignoring the true God, their contemporaries not only did not know whom to worship or how; everything else in society — morality, art, literature, politics — was skewed.

Hence Christians were unwilling to bend the knee when they heard the sound of the horn, pipe, lyre, trigon, harp, drum, and entire musical ensemble. Their task, however, unlike that of Shadrach, Meshach, and Abednego, was intellectual. They not only made confession, they set out to persuade others that they could love God more ardently and cleave to God more fervently if they sought God alone without the succor of rites that do not purify the soul. In doing so they laid the foundations for a new kind of society, one in which serving God faithfully was the highest duty.

Of course it was easy for Christians to criticize pagan religion with its many gods, its veneration of objects of wood and stone and gold, its divining and use of auguries and portents, and most of all its practice of animal sacrifice. Even pagan thinkers were critical of the practices that defined religious devotion in the cities; before the rise of Christianity there was a well-established tradition of criticism of religion in the ancient world. Philosophical religion, however, was another matter entirely, for many teachings were compatible with Christian theology. Augustine, it will be remembered, was helped in his move to the Catholic faith by reading the *libri Platonici,* which meant the books of the neo-Platonists, Porphyry and Plotinus. Yet Christian thinkers, including Augustine, were no less critical of the theological ideas of the philosophers than they were of the religious practices of their fellow citizens.

Although the philosophers had an intuition of the true God, in the view of Christian thinkers, they did not know how to serve God. In a mordant passage in *The City of God,* Augustine, chiding Porphyry for proclaiming his devotion to the God of the Hebrews while venerating lesser gods, cites the words from Exodus: "Anyone who sacrifices to other gods instead of to the Lord alone will be extirpated." Augustine's argument is that worship is to be offered only to God, for "God himself is the source of our bliss, . . . the goal of our striving."[25]

It has sometimes been argued that in *The City of God*, his apology "contra paganos," Augustine made place for a neutral secular space that could accommodate paganism and promote a "coherence of wills" about things relevant to this mortal life. Here the city of God could join hands with the earthly city for the cultivation of the arts of civilization. But for Augustine a neutral secular space could only be a society without God, subject to the *libido dominandi,* the lust for power. He was convinced that even this fallen world could have no genuine peace or justice unless society honored the one supreme God. There can be, he writes, no association of men united by a common sense of right where there is no true justice, and there can be no justice where God is not honored. "When a man does not serve God, what amount of justice are we to suppose exists in his being?" Where a people has no regard for God, there can be no social bond, no common life, and no virtue. "Although the virtues are reckoned by some people to be genuine and honorable when they are related only to themselves and are sought for no other end, even then they are puffed up and proud, and so are to be accounted vices rather than virtues."[26]

In *The City of God* Augustine is an apologist neither for a secular public space nor for theism. His great book is a defense of the worship of the one true God, the God who was acknowledged in ancient Israel, revealed in Christ, and venerated in the church. Like other early Christian apologists, he realized that it was not enough to make vague appeals to transcendent reality, to the god of philosophers, to a deity that takes no particular form in human life. The God of theism has no life independent of the practice of religion, of those who know God in prayer and devotion, who belong to a community of memory, and are bound together in common service. Only people schooled in the religious life, people like Shadrach, Meshach, and Abednego, can tell the difference between serving the one God faithfully and bowing down to idols. For Augustine defense of the worship of the true God inevitably required a defense of the church, the city of God as it exists in time.

---

25. Augustine, *De Civitate Dei* 10.41.
26. Ibid., 19.21, 25.

Eliot's *Christianity and Culture* admonishes us to take up the challenge of conceiving anew a Christian society. By this he did not mean a society that was composed solely of Christians, but one in which human life is ordered to ends that are befitting the true God. "It would be a society in which the natural end of man — virtue and well-being in community — is acknowledged for all, and the supernatural end — beatitude — for those who have the eyes to see it."[27] Only God can give ultimate purpose to our lives and direction to our society. The first commandment is not just a text to be memorized in catechism class; it is the theological basis for a just and human society.

I am reminded of a story I heard years ago in Germany when Walter Ulbricht, the German Communist leader, was head of the DDR. It was said that Ulbricht once had a conversation with Karl Barth about the new society that was being built in East Germany. Ulbricht boasted to Barth that the Communists would be teaching the ten commandments in the schools and that the precepts of the decalogue would provide the moral foundation for the new society. Barth listened politely and then said, "I have only one question, Herr Minister. Will you also be teaching the first commandment?"

27. Eliot, *Christianity and Culture*, p. 27.

Keeping the Faith: An Orthodox Perspective — An Essay on the Ascetic Character of Christian Theological Method

Kenneth Paul Wesche

Introduction

Many, if not all, of the religious schemes passing themselves off today as a renovated Christianity made relevant are nothing more than the redressing of themes already rejected by the church under different disguise. For example, teachers of the various second-century gnostic sects passed themselves off as bearers of a secret mystical knowledge of metaphysical reality that they set against the teaching of the institutional great church. Interestingly, the compelling proof that they offered as verification of their particular teaching was a claim to religious *experience,* or an encounter with the divine. Today experience is no less venerated by the many, and so those movements that can claim a knowledge derived from spiritual experience — whether New Age, the occult, revivalism, or pentecostal charismatic — exert a powerful attraction to the experientially hungry.

While a handful of the philosophically enlightened of antiquity viewed the different cults as the empty superstition of a vulgar populace, many viewed them as a crude yet real manifestation of the innate yearning in the human soul for the infinite, and respected the cultic rituals under certain qualifications. Consider, for example, Socrates' benign observance of his native religious rites,[1]

---

1. Plato, *Phaedo* 118: "Crito," said Socrates just before he died, "we ought to offer a cock to Asclepius. See to it and don't forget." In *Plato: Collected*

and the philosophical discussion Plotinus offered to account for the true cause of the apparent influence of the stars on one's destiny,[2] or his positive discussion on divination,[3] or his philosophical affirmation of the cults of Zeus and Aphrodite.[4] The same views are evident among the philosophically enlightened of today, who view the different religions of the world either as empty superstition or as the varied expression of the divine's universal manifestation. All religions therefore carry a relative validity as so many responses to the one divine being who is the vital spark hidden in the depths of human being and that all peoples therefore know intuitively.

Some Christian theologians have sought to elevate Christianity's crude absoluteness to the same level of sophistication found in the relativism so cherished now by the academic elite. Like the gnostic teachers of antiquity, they have therefore imagined a "Christ" that they believe can be studied meaningfully apart from any absolute identity with Jesus of Nazareth. Rather, Jesus of Nazareth is merely one of the human vessels in whom the "Christ" has manifested "itself." This "Christ" that their imaginations have produced is set up on the altar of their intellectual cult and worshiped as the name of whatever principle of reality their philosophical imagination has concocted. The resulting Christian relativism appears refreshingly benevolent in its tolerance, not only of other religions but even of existing divisions within the Christian church, as so many Christian responses to the "Christ's" manifestation in Jesus. Yet this "tolerance" effectively disguises a cunning, vicious hostility to any serious effort to work toward an authentic Christian unity whose goal is to bear witness in teaching and in praxis to the historical, particular person of Jesus of Nazareth as himself the risen Christ and Lord God, the Son of God, the only begotten Word of the Father who was in the beginning with God and who is God.

The relativism, together with its concomitant religious pluralism, that one encounters today is therefore nothing new. Over the

---

Dialogues, ed. Edith Hamilton and Huntington Cairns, (Princeton: Princeton Univ. Press, 1978), p. 98.

2. Plotinus *Enneads* 2.3.10-14.

3. Ibid., 3.3.6.

4. Ibid., 3.5.8.

centuries, however, this pagan relativism has discovered a subtly different and effective tactic in its attack on the church. The seductive pull of the ancient gnostics lay in the experience of true "knowledge" that they could offer of the true God. The philosophically enlightened theists of times past based their tolerance of different religions on the assumption that the Good One manifested "itself" to different peoples according to their cultural circumstances and could be "known" under different forms. But the pagan Christian pluralists of today seek to undermine the integrity of the gospel by working precisely from the distinctive Jewish and Christian conviction that affirms that God, because his essence lies outside even the intellectual and spiritual order, cannot be known as he is. Pointing out the apophatic character of Christian theology, they dismiss the traditional teachings of the church that have been revered as the deposit of divine revelation, and maintain that they are the product of culturally conditioned, human religious imagination.

The resulting scorn of Catholic tradition, for example, has gone so far as to challenge such bedrock convictions as the divinity of the particular Person of Jesus of Nazareth or the one time, particular incarnation of the divine Word of God as the *man* Jesus of Nazareth. Following from this rejection of the church's christological confession, the identity of God as Father, Son, and Holy Spirit is likewise dismissed as an unwarranted embellishment of Christian religious imagination. How can such claims as the divinity of Jesus or the consubstantiality of the Son and the Holy Spirit with the Father be held as absolutely true and nonnegotiable when God's essence lies beyond all human categories and cannot be comprehended by human thought? Church dogma is clearly the projection of culturally conditioned human ideas onto the infinite expanse that has passed under the name of God, and Jesus of Nazareth is the man whom Christian exuberance has deified far out of proportion to what is reasonable or believable on the grounds of natural physics or common sense.

Having rejected the conviction and teaching of the ancient church that God can be fully known on the church's own principle of God's supracomprehensible character, modern Christian theologians have shaken off the shackles of ecclesiastical tyranny. They now can get on with the task of establishing new "models" of God.

On the basis of these humanly produced models of God, they have generated the necessary space for erecting new models of Christ, of humanity, of ecclesiology, and of soteriology — which, when examined more closely, reveal themselves by their philosophical suppositions to be the same pagan tenets that in times past have repeatedly donned the vestments of Christian doctrine in the vain hope of finding a place at the Holy Bridegroom's marriage feast. Confused and disoriented by the rational seductiveness of this pagan Christian assault, many of the faithful, while they desperately strive to resist what they intuitively believe to be contrary to the gospel, have fallen into a state of helpless confusion. They are unsettled by those hostile claims that derive their justification precisely from a fundamental tenet of Christian theology: that God is uncreated and in his essence lies outside the comprehension of the created and culturally conditioned human mind.

The modern version of the claim that we cannot know God as he is is the inevitable result of the marriage in modern Western religious philosophy between the cosmology of biblical Judaism and the scientific methodology of Greek philosophy. Greek philosophy proceeds on the cosmological model that it inherited from pagan religion. God is either the Good or the One at the uppermost reaches of the cosmos where he cannot be described within the categories of "material" reality, or God is the living force that moves the cosmos, or God is the essential reality or stuff that all things are discovered to be when analyzed down to their underlying essence. Common to all of these variations is the unity of the cosmos, which includes "God" as its fundamental or constitutive component. The epistemological method this inspires is a process of abstraction, analogy, or deduction by which one finally arrives at the summit of the cosmos, where one encounters the One as It is. Philosophical or scientific enquiry proceeding by this method therefore can attain a real knowledge of God, for the mind conducting the enquiry is, in its essence, from the same realm within the cosmos as the One.

The Christian faith, however, derives its theology from biblical Judaism, whose cosmology offers a significantly different feature. The entire cosmos is the creation of the almighty, uncreated God. God's "throne" therefore lies outside the cosmos altogether. That is, God not only transcends the "material" order but also the "spiritual" or "intellective" order. The human being, even in his highest part, the intellect, can therefore never claim to exist on the same level as God. Even in the intellect a human being is a *creature* along with all other spiritual and intellectual substances. Within the cosmos, the heavens declare the glory of God and the firmament shows forth his handiwork (Ps. 19:1; 97:6), but the glory that is displayed reveals only his "back parts."[5] God does indeed dwell in the cosmos, but as he chooses, and he does so by descending and entering into it from his throne, which encompasses the cosmos *from outside.*

God's descent sheds forth the light in which the Christian faith affirms that we can know God as he is. The church from the beginning has proclaimed with the conviction of experiential knowledge that "God is the Lord and has revealed Himself to us; blessed is He who comes in the Name of the Lord!" This is what the church proclaims to the world every morning in the prayers of Matins. It is what she confesses with joy and thanksgiving at every divine liturgy immediately on partaking of the holy gifts: "We have seen the true Light, we have received the heavenly Spirit, we have found the true faith, worshipping the undivided Trinity who has saved us!" These announcements derive from the reality of holy illumination, that is, holy baptism, in which the believer is clothed with nothing less than Christ himself — "As many as have been baptized into Christ, have put on Christ!" — who is the wisdom of God who makes the unknowable Father known (John 1:18). The gift of illumination enables the Christian to pray with a confident hope at the conclusion of the hourly prayers: "Encompass us round about with Thy holy angels that we may attain to the unity of the faith and to the *comprehension* of Thine *incomprehensible* glory."

We can attain unity of faith because God the Father has revealed himself truly in his Son: "He who has seen me has seen the Father." We can comprehend the Father even in his incomprehensibility because of the mystery of the only begotten Son's dispensation in which the most holy and pure Virgin Mother of God contained in her womb the uncontainable One; her body was made more spacious than the heavens, for her womb was made the throne

5. Cf. Gregory of Nazianzus, *Theological Oration* 2.3; *Patrologiae Graecae* 36, col. 29 AB.

of the King of all in whom all things move and have their being, in whom all things came to be and in whom all things cohere.

The fact that "He who is who He is" utterly transcends the human intellect and the cosmos means, however, that the Greek scientific method cannot work as a means of coming to know the true, living God. The epistemological method of Greek philosophy takes one only to the summit of the cosmos, and there one has found only the outermost edge of the cosmos, which is not God. When one assumes the Judeo-Christian cosmology, the inevitable result of endeavoring to discover the real God by means of the scientific method of Greek cosmology will be, at best, a severance of faith and knowledge, faith being the blind, stubborn conviction that God is, and knowledge being that which can be scientifically demonstrated (a position represented by the "Christian" philosophers of the "Enlightenment"). At worst the result will be a stubborn atheism in which God is nothing more than the projection of humanity onto the infinite (Ludwig Feuerbach). The only philosophically responsible alternative is agnosticism. The Christian faith has taught the philosophy that what one encounters at the height of human intellectual discourse is not God, but only the height of human intellectual discourse.[6]

In this introduction I have described the difficulty that the following reflections are seeking to address. This difficulty consists in the Christian claim that the uncreated God who lies outside the cosmos and the intellectual order of the human mind can still be known as he is. Thus, on the basis of this conviction, Christian theology maintains that the tenets fundamental to catholic Christian doctrine — chiefly the incarnation of God the Word as Jesus of Nazareth, and the identity of God as Father, Son, and Holy Spirit — are *not* human productions, but divinely revealed truths and are thereby nonnegotiable. The following observations, therefore, turn first to reflect on the experience of biblical Judaism and of early Christianity in order to demonstrate that the direct and immediate knowledge of God is an experience fundamental to the Christian

6. Etiénne Gilson made the same point in "God and Contemporary Thought," chap. 4 of *God and Philosophy* (New Haven: Yale Univ. Press, 1942), pp. 109-43.

faith. The experience of God as revealed in the experience of biblical Judaism and early Christianity help to make comprehensible the properly ascetic character of Christian theological method, and the presentation and description of Christian theology's ascetic character is the aim toward which I am moving in this essay. Only by understanding the fundamental experience of the Christian faith can one understand that the method of Christian religious philosophy, by which the true and living God is known as he is, cannot at heart be the inferential process of Greek science but must be the ascetic attitude of humility, repentance, and contrition.

The Biblical Jewish Root of the Church

If the vine that is the Christian faith grew from the soil of the Old Testament, the leaves and blossoms of the vine itself bear the shape and coloring of Jewish apocalyptic. Broadly speaking, Jewish apocalyptic refers to revelations concerning God's intervention in human events bringing about the end of history, the eschaton. The vision of Jewish apocalyptic is central to the thought and praxis of the church. Even when the church spread into a Greek cultural milieu and began to express herself in the terms of Hellenistic philosophical thought, the structure determining the content of her theological expression was that of Jewish apocalyptic. So primary is this structure to the shape of the Christian faith that when theological thought is loosed from its Jewish apocalyptic orientation, the presentation and disposition of what is purported to be the "Christian faith" becomes a syncretistic mishmash of alien ideologies and religious experiences that may hold a seductively sweet attraction, but that are wholly devoid of the uncreated healing power and resurrected life of Jesus Christ, the uncreated and ever-existing Son of God.

The principle themes of Jewish apocalyptic that are determinative for the church are themselves, however, drawn from biblical Judaism. Rehearsing the interconnection of apocalyptic and biblical themes brings to light the fundamental conviction of the Christian faith that God is the Lord and has revealed himself to us; blessed is he who comes in the Name of the Lord!

The Sovereignty of God

A fundamental feature of biblical Judaism is the absolute sovereignty of God over all aspects of Jewish life. The God who is sovereign over Israel is not some abstract, universal concept; it is quite misleading simply to say that Israel worshiped the one God, as though Israel conceived of God in the same abstract terms as the Greek pagan philosophers. The God of Israel is a particular God among other gods, who appeared to Abraham, Isaac, and Jacob. The God of Israel has therefore a particular personality that distinguishes him from other gods. The election of Abraham and his descendants as the particular people of this particular God brought the people of Israel into being and established their culture, for they believed that God gave them the laws and ordinances that shaped their culture.

Accordingly, apart from the God who chose them and set up their social existence, Israel would have no distinctive character and would not even exist. That is, Israel's continued existence as a nation, the vitality of his culture, and the distinctive character of his identity were utterly dependent on the mercy and life-giving power of his particular God. The prophets therefore repeatedly warned Israel that following after the gods of other nations and submitting to their worship was to neglect the Lord God's commands and to reject his absolute sovereignty over Israel. This was nothing less for Israel than suicide, for God is the source of Israel's life and identity; to turn away from him is to spurn the source of Israel's life and identity and to bring about Israel's total destruction as a nation. Not only Israel's existence, but his fate as well is governed by the Lord God: If Israel is obedient to the Lord God of Abraham, *he* will give them life; if Israel is disobedient, *he* will send their destruction on them. The ruins of Israel will testify therefore to the power of the Lord God who gives life and who destroys, and to his intense jealousy for the honor of his Name.

Within the context of the Lord God's absolute sovereignty, the initiatory rite of circumcision receives its character as more than an entrance into the fellowship of Israel. It seals one's entrance into a society whose existence, character, and identity is received wholly from the God of Abraham, Isaac, and Jacob, and it presupposes acceptance and total submission to the divine ordinances, laws, and precepts from which Israel receives his existence and life.

Hidden within the attitude of submission to the sovereign Lord God is a fundamental conviction of biblical Judaism: God himself is present at the heart of authentic Israelite culture. That is, when one gets beyond the cultural and cultic forms of Israelite society, one encounters the living God himself. At the heart of biblical Judaism, in her law, her cultic prescriptions, and the word of her prophets, the reality one encounters is not human religious imagination or a codified law written by Mosaic scribes and claimed to be given by God in order to secure the allegiance of the people. God himself dwells in the midst of Israel, and it is his presence that makes Israel a "holy nation." The high priest of Israel entered the inmost altar of the temple only once a year — not because Israel liked to *pretend* that God was present there, nor because they believed that the death of the seventy men of Bethshemesh who dared look into the Ark of the Lord was an accident (1 Sam. 6:19-20). They believed that the One who stood in Israel's midst and gave to him his terrible vitality was the Lord God himself. He made the inner altar the *Holy* of Holies; he made the Ark of the Covenant a sacred object that could not be profaned.

The living presence of God in the heart of authentic Israelite culture, that is, in Israel's laws and ordinances, explains why the Psalmist so loved the law and ordinances of God. They were sweet to him, a joy to keep and a light to one's path, because the Lord God of Israel was present in them. His presence gave to them their sweetness, their joy, and their light; to keep the law accordingly was to enter into the presence of the living God himself. The life that one lived by keeping the law was the life of the Lord God himself, and the character of that life was the character of the Lord God himself. Biblical theology is therefore not *produced* but *received* from the God of Abraham himself. Accordingly, authentic biblical theology is of a particular character, for it is a description of the particular Lord God who stands at the heart of biblical worship, who has brought Israel into being and given to him his distinctive character and identity.

The Salvation of God

To say that the Lord God of Israel is not an abstract concept but a particular God is to indicate that he is "substantive" and "concrete" (or, in the truly ecumenical language of the church, he is *hypostatic*). His particular character likewise therefore is not an abstract concept, but substantive with concrete effects; that is, the effects of God's character are active and visible in this world of time and space, and they are so precisely because he is the Creator and Lord of time and space. Since they are the concrete effects of his character, the acts of God demonstrate who he is and what he is like.

The central event in Israel's history that demonstrates the character of his God is the *Pascha* of the Exodus. The redemption of the Israelites from their Egyptian bondage was initiated and accomplished wholly by the Lord God (Deut. 26:8). The sons of Israel were utterly helpless against the might of Pharoah and in no position to mount any kind of effective, armed resistance. Moses did not fight the Pharoah; he did not bring on the plagues, slay the first-born of the Egyptians, part the Red Sea, or discomfit the chariots and horsemen of Pharoah's army; nor did he produce the pillar of cloud by day and the pillar of fire by night, or send down the manna from heaven. All of this was accomplished by God. Moses simply passed on the directives of God to the Israelites in order to prepare them for their deliverance, and the Israelites simply did what they were told.

The *Pascha* of the Exodus demonstrated concretely for the Israelites that of all the descriptions they could give of their God, almighty Savior was the highest. This God was almighty Savior because his power extended not only over Israel but even over the gods of Egypt and the powerful Pharoah. As they took possession of the land of Canaan, the victories won by Israel's mighty heroes — Joshua, Gideon, Samson, David, and Jonathan — demonstrated that anyone who was righteous, who was faithful to the ordinances of this particular God, was filled with the sovereign power and life of that God and thereby enabled to conquer foes who in appearance were many times mightier than were the Israelites.

These experiences taught Israel that his particular God was the mightiest God on earth: "What god is so great as our God? You are the God who works wonders" (Ps. 77:13-14). Later, the prophets came to know him as the only true, living God; the gods of the other nations were either helpless *daemones* against the God of Israel, or empty idols devoid even of the power of speech, deriving their existence from the hands of human craftsmen, wholly deserving of scorn and derision. The *Pascha* of the Exodus is therefore the concrete event that demonstrates in a conclusive way the saving character of God and the full extent of his sovereignty and power.

But more than that, the saving acts of God demonstrate concretely the fundamental fact of Israel's existence: God himself is in the midst of Israel acting for Israel's salvation. In the midst of the Exodus, God himself stands among the Israelites, watching over their flight; while Moses guides the people to the Red Sea, the Lord God goes before them and parts the waters so Israel can pass, and at the same time he covers Israel's flanks and routs the Egyptian army while Israel passes through the sea as on dry ground.

The living presence of God himself in the laws and ordinances of Israelite culture transfigures the annual *paschal* ordinance from a mere commemoration of a past event into a "vigil to be kept for the Lord by all the Israelites throughout their generations" (Exod. 12:42). In this annual observance, the faithful Israelite watches for the coming of the same Lord God who delivered Israel from the hands of the Egyptians, so that in the *paschal* ordinance itself, the faithful Israelite stands before the same living God who accomplished the first *Pascha*. He is thereby truly united to the first *Pascha*, for he stands directly in the same divine reality that was present there and gave to it its true meaning. Yet it is more than that, for the God whom the faithful Israelite encounters in the *paschal* ordinance is the same Lord God who gave the law to Moses, who called Abraham and entered into covenant with him, who brought the heavens and the earth into being and made man from the dust of the ground, who spoke to the prophets, and — from the Christian perspective — who in these last days was incarnate of the Virgin Mary and who became man, who suffered, died, and was buried and who rose again on the third day accomplishing the true mystical *Pascha*. Thus the *paschal* ordinance is not a dry, human remembrance but a *divine* ordinance, an entrance into the divine reality of God's heavenly kingdom, wherein one is united to the whole history of Israel and the meaning of all creation, for one stands in the presence of the very God who called all things into being and established the nation of Israel as a particular people with a particular identity and character.

This explains why the *paschal* ordinance is exclusive to circumcised Israelites.[7] Because the living God is present in the ordinance of the *Pascha,* and because one stands directly before him in the *paschal* ordinance, no one may partake of the *paschal* supper "safely" if one has not first sealed one's total submission to the sovereignty of the Lord God by accepting the Abrahamic rite of circumcision. If one does not enter that community brought into being by the Lord God and accept the mantle of the divine commandments that give character and life to that community, one partakes unworthily and to his condemnation, for he is still an Egyptian dabbling in the service of other gods. For the prophets, this is the attitude not only of the Gentile but also of the Israelite who dishonors the demands of his circumcision by following after other gods (see Isa. 1:11-15; Amos 5:21-24).

The Israelite who partakes of the *paschal* ordinance even while following after other gods insults the sovereign majesty of the Lord God by placing him on the same level with other gods. He muddies the purity of the Lord's covenant by smearing it with the filth of his allegiance to the pagan gods. This person embraces the scorn of the proud, the contempt of those who are at ease; for by believing that one can enjoy the benefits of God's saving power in celebrating the *paschal* ordinance and yet escape the demands of God's absolute sovereignty by following after the pleasures of Egypt, one arrogantly exalts the convenient demands of human laziness and ignorance over the commands of God. Such a person is not watching for the

---

7. See Exod. 12:43-49:

And the Lord said to Moses and Aaron, "This is the ordinance of the passover: no foreigner shall eat of it but every slave that is bought for money may eat of it after you have circumcised him. No sojourner or hired servant may eat of it. . . . All the congregation of Israel shall keep it. And when a stranger shall sojourn with you and would keep the passover to the Lord, let all his males be circumcised, then he may come near and keep it. But no uncircumcised person shall eat of it."

Lord God who comes in the *paschal* ordinance and so does not see what the faithful Israelite has seen in obedience to Yahweh: that the Lord God of Israel is not one to dabble with.

Israel's God is not like the other gods; indeed, there is no other god before him. No god can stand against him. He is the One who rides on the clouds as on a chariot, who makes the heavens to roll up like a scroll, who calls forth and they are created. The whole earth is his and all that is in it. At his rebuke the mighty waters of chaos flee; he sets the bound beyond which they cannot pass. At his command the mountains rise and the valleys sink down to the place where he appoints for them. The great sea monsters look to him for their food in its season, for he is the Lord God of all. He does not tolerate arrogance or injustice or deception or any kind of wickedness, but he demands absolute obedience in humility, contrition of heart, purity, justice, and mercy. He will abundantly pardon those who turn to him with their whole heart, but he will destroy those who sneer at him and go after other gods, together with their gods.

The *paschal* ordinance therefore stoutly forbids the uncircumcised to partake precisely because the Lord God himself is present in the ordinance, and one dare not approach him unworthily or profane the sanctity of his Name. All of this points to the fundamental conviction that within the laws and ordinances that give character to Israelite culture, one comes directly before the living God himself, not before mere human customs or religious traditions. In these terms, the "covenant" of the *paschal* ordinance that is central to the life of biblical Judaism is not primarily a commemoration of God's mighty, saving deeds; it is primarily an act of worship by which one enters into the presence of the living God of Abraham, Isaac, and Jacob. There the faithful Israelite recounts the Lord's mighty deeds, either in joyful gratitude or in pious lament, asking God directly — because God is present — to act again in the present as he has in the past.

These are the major themes of biblical Judaism that nourish the cosmic, eschatological vision of Jewish apocalyptic. Within this context, the early church understood the significance of Jesus' identity and the New Covenant or New Testament that he has accomplished.

The Jewish Apocalyptic Vision

The Cosmic Scope of the Lord God's Sovereignty

Adam and Eve's disobedience gave birth immediately to the death that God had warned them of when he said, "In the day that you eat of [the tree of the knowledge of good and evil] you shall die" (Gen. 2:17). Because Jewish thought knows God as "the living God" who is God of the living, not of the dead, it views death in its essence as being cut off from God.[8] Its fruit, therefore, is separation and disintegration. Accordingly, the word of God to Adam and Eve proved true, for on the very day that they disobeyed God, they who before had been lover and beloved separated themselves from one another when they became enemy and accuser. Then they, who had been created in the very image of God, were separated from their Creator and from their original home when they were expelled from the Garden. Cut off from their Creator, the "fountain of life" (Ps. 36:7-9), Adam and Eve were left to their own "vital" resources. Their eventual disintegration into the dust whence they were brought into being was now inevitable, for they could draw only from the "nothing" out of which they were brought into being at God's creative command.[9] Hence, the separation of death is complete: Cut off from God and separated from one another, the human being finally is separated even from the self in the separation of soul and body, and in the disintegration of the body into dust.

If one considers humankind's disobedience from the perspective of God's creative intention, the resulting dissolution into death can appear not only as a tragedy for human dignity but even as an affront to the divine majesty. According to the vision of 1 Enoch, written sometime in the first century B.C., "Men were created to be like angels, permanently to maintain pure and righteous lives. Death, which destroys everything, would not have touched them, had it not been through their knowledge by which they shall perish;

8. See Hans Walter Wolff, *Anthropology of the Old Testament* (Philadelphia: Fortress, 1974), p. 106.
9. Cf. St. Athanasius *De Incarnatione* 5.

death is now eating us by this power."[10] In other words, God's intention in creating humans is that they should live forever like the angels, in holiness and sanctity of life. Our disobedience, together with its companion death, threatens the divine intention with failure. The power of death threatens to usurp God's absolute dominion over everything by wresting the whole of creation from the divine intention and binding it fast to its own terrible lordship. It thus makes for itself a domain where God's might and avenging justice apparently cannot reach.

For the unrighteous, death is not the ultimate punishment, even as for the righteous it is the ultimate grief; for there in the depths of Sheol, while the righteous mourn their separation from God, the unrighteous might find some consolation in believing that they have escaped the terror of facing God's wrath and vindication. The pride of disobedience and the power of death therefore stand before the throne of the almighty God in scoffing hauteur, mocking the sovereignty of God. They have apparently undermined the divine intention, for the righteous die and the unrighteous have found an escape from the judgment of God. Moreover, the unrighteous are found to suffer no worse than the righteous, for both descend into the same dreary depths of Sheol. The gates to Paradise, humankind's true home, have been closed to the righteous as well as to the unrighteous, and there is no way even for the righteous to reenter. Unrighteousness has gotten off "scott free." Since death is the end for all, both righteous and unrighteous, why not make the best of it? Eat, drink, and be merry, for tomorrow we die! You only go around once in life; so grab for all the gusto you can!

In the vision of Jewish apocalyptic, the saving power that the Lord God demonstrated in all the signs and wonders surrounding the *Pascha* of the Exodus concretely reveal that there are no limits to God's absolute sovereignty. "If Yahweh alone is God, the recognition cannot be wanting that even death cannot secure any sphere of sovereignty into which Yahweh is incapable of penetrating."[11] From this conviction, there arises in Jewish apocalyptic the belief

10. James H. Charlesworth, ed., *Old Testament Pseudepigrapha* (New York: Doubleday, 1983), 1:48.

11. Wolff, *Anthropology*, pp. 108, 110.

that the unrighteous cannot escape God even in death, whereas "life cannot end in death for the [righteous] man for whom God himself has become the subsistence of life (Ps 73.27f.)."[12]

The Expectation of the Jewish Apocalyptic Vision

The apocalyptic hope in divine vindication of the righteous and punishment of the unrighteous centers on the expectation of a particular Someone whose appearing is expected to mark the end of history and the final judgment of the world. The pseudepigraphic literature calls this eschatological Someone the "Righteous One," the "Holy One," the "Elect One." Early Christian exegesis traces this apocalyptic vision of a Someone to come in the texts of the Old Testament, where references to a coming Someone run through the disparate texts as a continuous thread, binding them into one continuous fabric and progressively weaving into the fabric's warp and woof a portrait of this Someone.

For instance, at the very moment when Adam and Eve realized that what they had done could lead to despair, God gives hope in the curse he pronounces on the serpent: "I will put enmity between you and the woman, and between your offspring and hers; he will strike your head, and you will strike his heel" (Gen. 3:15). From the perspective of early Christian exegesis, the bleak dawn of human history is pierced with the divine ray of hope. History proceeds from a foundation of hope in the appearing of a Someone, a child of Eve, who will destroy the serpent and heal the separation from God effected by human sin. Buried in the curse of the serpent, however, is a bitter indication that the child of Eve will himself suffer death even as he destroys the serpent; for to be bruised on the heel by a serpent can refer only to a fatal, venomous bite.

Yahweh's oath to Abraham following the sacrifice of Isaac on Mt. Moriah contains an enigmatic reference to a Someone as the "seed" of Abraham: "Your seed shall possess the gate of his enemies, and in your seed shall all the nations of the earth be blessed" (Gen. 22:17f.). As in the curse of the serpent, so here,

12. Ibid., p. 109.

too, one finds allusion to some kind of conflict between Abraham's "seed" and his enemies. The curse of the serpent leaves in doubt the final end of the Someone in his victory over the serpent. Here, however, is a clear indication that his end will be an unmitigated triumph, for "he will possess the gate of his enemies" — a Hebraism denoting total victory for the aggressor if he has gained complete control of the fortifying walls protecting his enemy's city. Moreover, the beneficient influence of this Someone's victory will extend far beyond the parochial walls of Israel; it will encompass "all nations." The Someone to come is thereby portrayed as one whose appearing will be of universal significance. The death of the Someone hinted at in the serpent's curse is difficult to reconcile with the expectations raised in the covenant with Abraham, but taken together, the two covenants indicate that somehow his death will prove to be not only the destruction of the serpent and victory over the "enemy" but also the source of blessing to "all nations."

Further details are added to the portrait of the Someone to come in Moses' final address to the Israelites: He will be "like Moses" (Deut. 18:18). The expectation of a second Moses suggests to early Christian midrash that the Someone to come will, like Moses, be a revealer of God's Name, a giver of God's law, a redeemer from a mighty pharoah, a leader through a wilderness, even an intercessor for the people who lays down his own life for the salvation of his people (Exod. 32:32).[13]

In Nathan's prophecy to King David, the Someone to come is described further as a Davidic scion coming from David's royal line whose kingdom shall have no end (2 Sam. 7:12-16). The theme of suffering, which was sounded in Genesis, returns in Nathan's prophecy with the explanation that its cause will lie in the iniquity committed by the Son of David (2 Sam 7:14).

Without question, modern exegetes may justifiably maintain that the Someone referred to in each of these prophecies was believed by the parties immediately involved to be Isaac, then Joshua, and

---

13. Cf. the *Paschal Homily* of Melito of Sardis. Greek text and English translation in *Melito of Sardis on Pascha: Oxford Early Christian Texts,* ed. Stuart George Hall (London: Oxford Univ. Press/Clarendon Press, 1979).

then Solomon. But early Christian exegesis could point out that not one of them satisfied the high expectations raised in these prophecies. Isaac died an old man, and one can hardly say that he had any major conflict with an enemy whose gates he could boast of possessing. Even if one understands "seed" collectively to refer to Israel (and St. Paul is quite clear that it is singular, referring prophetically to Jesus Christ; Gal. 3:16f.), one can hardly say that the Israelites enjoyed more than a temporary possession of their enemies' gates. As great as Joshua was in leading Israel across the Jordan into the Promised Land, he still did not match the greatness of Moses. Moses, after all, a mere shepherd, had by God's power overcome the mightiest god on earth, the Pharoah, and single-handedly wrested the Israelites from his power. Joshua's success in Canaan, on the other hand, was marginal at best. The idolatrous nations occupying Canaan were not entirely rooted out, and the integrity of Israel's devotion to Yahweh was continually compromised in Israel's subsequent history. One should not wonder, then, that the Israelites continued to look for "the prophet" like Moses even after Joshua's great legacy had been completed. Although Solomon became a legend in Hebraic lore, his kingdom came to an end. If God's Word is true, then there must be another to whom these prophecies refer beyond Isaac, or Joshua, or Solomon.

Ezekiel gives intriguing but puzzling indications that the Someone to come will be God himself, who will come to shepherd his flock, Israel (Ezek. 34:11-16). The same passage, however, identifies this One also as David the King returning to Israel to establish him in righteousness and to teach him the law of God (Ezek. 34:23).

Deutero-Isaiah's vision of the "Servant of Yahweh" sent by God as a "light to the nations" (Isa. 49) takes up the disparate threads laid down in the curse of the serpent and in God's words to Abraham, Moses, and David and weaves them together into one coherent portrait of the Someone to come. Like Moses, he is the "Servant of Yahweh." His appearing will mark Israel's deliverance from the unrighteous, and his everlasting salvation. The prophetic vision that sees the return of the righteous to Zion in the midst of world peace and prosperity (Isa. 51) calls to mind the expulsion from the Garden and suggests that the gates to Eden — the heavenly Jerusalem — will be opened once again when the Servant appears.

The cosmic scope of the salvation brought by the Servant, which will reach to the ends of the earth (Isa. 49:6), recalls Yahweh's words to Abraham: "In your seed shall all nations of the earth be blessed."

These later prophetic visions, when joined to the vision found in the Pentateuch and in the historical books, produce a profound description of the Someone to come. If he is to be a second Moses, a second David, even God himself, then he is the leader and king of Israel — a description that, for the Christian exegete, would alone suggest his divine identity, since Israel has but one true King, the Lord God almighty. As the leader and king of Israel he must embody the entire nation in himself, and accordingly share in the nation's fortunes or misfortunes. Moses, for example, although himself a righteous man and innocent of Israel's rebellion, so identified with his people that, with them, he was prevented from entering the Promised Land. Seen within the ancient Hebraic theology of king-ship, then, the "iniquity" for which the second David will be chas-tised and which will be the cause of his suffering (2 Sam. 7:14) is in fact not his own. Rather, in Deutero-Isaiah's vision of the *Suffering* Servant, it is the "iniquity of us all." This context explains the notes of suffering and triumph implicit in the Adamic, Abrahamic, and Davidic portrayals of the Someone to come:

> Surely he has borne our griefs and carried our sorrows; yet we ourselves esteemed him stricken, smitten of God, and afflicted. But he was pierced through for our transgressions. He was crushed for our iniquities; the chastening for our well-being fell upon him, and by his scourging we are healed. All of us like sheep have gone astray, each of us has turned to his own way; but the Lord has caused the iniquity of us all to fall on him. (Isa. 53:4-6)

The purpose in drawing this sketch of Jewish apocalyptic has been to highlight what appears to me to lie at the heart of the apocalyptic vision: the coming of a divine Someone. If at the heart of biblical Judaism one stands in the presence of the almighty Lord God himself, at the heart of Jewish apocalyptic one encounters the absence of a divine Someone whose presence is imminent. The Jewish apocalyptic hope fills the *paschal* ordinance with a sense of anticipation; the "night of watching" is now a watching for the coming of God's "Elect Righteous One," who is expected to deliver the elect righteous ones from injustice and the inclusive power of death. The central experience of both biblical Judaism and Jewish apocalyptic is of a transcendent Someone, and the focus is on him. Everything else, including the narratives of God's mighty acts, is secondary to the presence or absence of the divine Someone who stands in the midst of Israel. This is the ethos in which the Christian church was born.

The Vision of the Church

The New Testament

Recalling the theocentric focus of biblical Judaism and of Jewish apocalyptic is essential for orienting the theological task properly on the divine reality that brought the Christian church into being and that gave to her her distinctive character and identity. Western Christians who protest against any kind of human magisterial authority have elevated the holy Scriptures as the sole authoritative judge that determines what is authentic to Christian belief. This view of Scripture raises a methodological problem, however, as well as a historical problem.

Any serious student of the Bible sooner or later discovers the fact that when the church first appeared, and in the more than one hundred years that followed her historical manifestation, there was no such thing as a closed scriptural canon. The church had access to scrolls containing the writings of our present Old Testament, believed to be holy and inspired, and several revered translations of the Hebrew Scriptures, but there was no canon as such until A.D. 120 when the rabbis closed the Torah, the Christian Old Testament. The "scriptures" to which Jesus and the apostles referred could include, beside the writings now forming the Old Testament, a great many other highly revered writings, such as those called the Old Testament Pseudepigrapha. These, too, were considered to be possessed of a certain divine inspiration, and continued to be highly regarded even after they failed to gain entrance into an official biblical canon.

An official New Testament canon did not exist for more than four hundred years of the church's historical manifestation. The first New Testament canon as such was formed only in the mid second century, and owed its formation to a certain heretic, Marcion, who had migrated to Rome from Asia Minor. An orthodox canon of the New Testament was put forth shortly thereafter, largely to uphold the divine inspiration and authentic apostolic stamp of other holy books excluded from Marcion's heretical canon.

This history, then, exposes the methodological problem in which one becomes entangled by upholding Scripture as the sole authority for determining Christian belief. Clearly, the authority for determining which holy writings were canonical and which were not was not the canon of Holy Scripture, for there was no such canon. Something else determined the canonicity of the writings. Obviously, the scriptural canon was formed within a certain context, and it was this context that was authoritative for determining what a particular Scripture meant and whether or not its meaning was true to the faith of the church. This suggests that the dictum "Scripture interprets itself" would make little sense to the early church, for in her experience, Scripture does not interpret itself: something else does, namely the context in which the Scriptures themselves were judged for their canonicity. To uphold Scripture as the supreme authority therefore closes one off to the ethos and experience of the early church that provided the context for understanding the Scriptures. One cannot accordingly understand the church or the Scriptures in the same way as the early church did; one approaches both Scripture and the early church from a context that is different, if not alien, to the ethos of the early church out of which Scripture itself emerged.[14]

Since there was no officially closed canon in the first one hundred years of the church's historical manifestation, it follows that in the mind of the ancient church, the terms "old" and "new testament" could not refer to a closed set of divinely inspired books; they had to refer to something or some*one* else. And in fact, in the writings of the New Testament itself, the term "new covenant" or

14. On this point, one can read further in John Meyendorff, *Living Tradition* (Crestwood, N.Y.: St. Vladimir's Seminary Press, 1978).

"new testament" refers to the Eucharist or, more specifically, to Jesus himself: "This cup is my blood of the New Covenant which is shed for you and for many. As often as you drink of it, do this in remembrance of me."[15] These words show us that in the New Covenant we are in the same climate as the Old Covenant, for we are not simply commemorating some divine person's mighty acts, we are standing in the presence of a divine Some*one,* Jesus himself, for the bread that is eaten and the cup that is drunk are made to become, by his living presence and by the descent of his Holy Spirit, his body and blood (John 6).

Most significantly, however, is the conviction of the church that in the New Covenant the believer is entering the heart of the Old Covenant and therefore stands in the presence of the Lord God of Israel who delivered Israel from the Egyptians. For in the presence of Jesus, one comes into the presence of the Father (John 14:10f.), and in the presence of the Father, one's eyes are opened to the real identity of Jesus of Nazareth: "Now we know [because we see — οιδαμεν]," say the disciples at the eucharistic gathering of the Last Supper, "that you know everything and that you have come from God" (John 16:29f.). That knowledge of Jesus' true identity is *seen* in the eucharistic worship of the church suggests that the Lord's response to Peter's confession ("Blessed are you Simon bar-Jonah, for flesh and blood have not revealed this to you, *but my Father who is in heaven*"; Matt. 16:16-18) also presupposes the eucharistic setting of the New Covenant.

Paul passed on to his converts the tradition that he had received from the Lord himself — the Eucharist. "I handed on to you what was given to me from the Lord Himself, that on the night He was betrayed, He took bread, and when He had given thanks — ευχαριστησας" (1 Cor. 11:23-24). Further, St. Ignatius greets the brethren in Philadelphia "in the blood of Jesus Christ,"[16] and his letter to the Smyrneans reveals the Eucharist as the source of real existence and the living power in which the bishop derives his ecclesial authority.

15. Cf. also Matt. 26:28 and par., 1 Cor. 11:25; 2 Cor. 3:6-14; Heb. 8:8-13; 9:15; 12:24 where "New Covenant" refers to the Eucharist.
16. St. Ignatius *Letter to the Philadelphians* 1.1.

These and many other texts demonstrate that in the mind of the early church the New Testament was the Eucharist, not a set of canonical scriptures. The Eucharist is the source of the church's knowledge, not because it is a commemoration of Jesus' passion and resurrection, but because it is the very flesh and blood of Jesus Christ.[17] In the celebration of the New Covenant, then, one stands in the living presence of Jesus Christ himself, and in him one stands in the presence of God his Father, the God of Israel. It is the vision of Jesus Christ in authentic eucharistic worship that bestows on the church, as on the disciples, the knowledge of Jesus as the Christ, the bearer of the Father's Holy Spirit, the perfect Icon and Word of the Father, the very Name of God, the Son of God in whom the Father almighty dwells, in whom the fullness of God dwells bodily, in whom one sees and knows the Father almighty and from whom one receives the gift of the Holy Spirit who "proceeds from the Father" (John 15:26).

The vision of the risen Christ is therefore received fully only in the faithful observance of the New Testament, that is, in the Eucharist. In the knowledge gained from this vision the church confesses this One who in his flesh is of the race of David, born of Mary, to be "in [his] will and in [his] power [terms that identify the 'seat' of his inmost being, or his 'inner man'], the Son of God,"[18] because his will and his power — in the later elaboration of Gregory the Theologian and Gregory of Nyssa — are the very will and power of the Father almighty.[19] The subjective experience of the church's eucharistic worship yields the objective criterion that itself determines the truth of subjective experience and all theological teaching.[20] In the words of St. Ignatius: "[Anyone] who does not confess

17. The letters of St. Ignatius, referred to above, written around A.D. 110, as well as the *Adversus Haer.* of Irenaeus of Lyons, written around 150-160, make it abundantly clear that the experience of the early church perceived the eucharistic elements to be the very flesh and blood of Jesus Christ, and this belief distinguished the "orthodox" from the schismatics and heretics.

18. St. Ignatius *Letter to the Smyrneans* 1.1.

19. For a fuller study of this point, see the study, "Triadological Shaping of Latin and Greek Christology," pt. 2, *Pro Ecclesia*, 2/1 (Winter 1993): 84-105.

20. "Our understanding," writes Irenaeus, "is a symphony with the Eucharist, and the Eucharist establishes our understanding." *Contra Haer.* 4.18.5, PG 7, col. 1028 AB.

that Our Lord Jesus was clothed in the flesh thereby denies Him completely and is clothed in a corpse."[21] Or in the words of St. John, "Beloved, whoever denies that Jesus is the Christ come in the flesh is not of God" (John 4:3).

By the objective criterion of this confession the church throughout her history has exposed and identified as heretical any teaching or practice that implicitly or explicitly denies the full humanity, the full divinity, *and* the divine personality of Jesus of Nazareth. Thus, the church has identified as heretical the notion that Jesus is a man endowed with a special grace of God, or that he is of a different essence than the Father, or that he is devoid of a human mind, or that he is a human person joined to the divine Person of the divine Logos, or that he is some kind of new Christic species possessed only of a divine will. These christological teachings are unfaithful to the knowledge of Jesus Christ received in her eucharistic worship.

Within the New Testament — the Eucharist — where one encounters the living and risen Lord Jesus Christ together with his Father and his Holy Spirit, the church celebrates the mighty act of Jesus that demonstrates the divine character of his sovereign power: his *Pascha*. The fourth-century Cappadocians drew from Scripture and from the tradition of the early Jewish-Christian "elders" to identify Jesus, the Son of God and the power of God, as the One who carries out the Father's commands, while the Holy Spirit is the One who perfects those commands.[22] This means that Jesus, whose *Pascha* we celebrate, is, in the church's confession, the very One who accomplished the Exodus in the power of the Father's Holy Spirit. To enter into the bosom of Jesus Christ and to enter into his *Pascha* is therefore to stand in the very reality that, in the vision of Jewish apocalyptic, the *Pascha* of the Exodus was all about: the concrete demonstration of God's absolute sovereignty and his power over all enemies, including death. Jesus the Christ has trampled down death by his own death, and has given life to those in the tombs by pouring out his Holy Spirit, the Lord and Giver of Life. The *Pascha* of Christ is therefore the consummation and perfection

21. St. Ignatius *Letter to the Smyrneans* 5.2.
22. Cf. "Triadological Shaping."

of the Old Covenant and the fulfillment of the Jewish apocalyptic hope. It is the supreme act to which all of his other mighty acts point — his giving sight to the blind, his authority to forgive sins, his power over the winds and the waters, the primeval forces of chaos — by which he proves himself to be the Son of God; for his acts reveal that he possesses the same character and the same power as God.

All of this illustrates the point that the church's reference point was the eschatological vision of Jewish apocalyptic, not a closed canon of New Testament writings. Since Jesus was the eschatological Someone looked for in Jewish apocalyptic and in the "old" testaments, the eschatological vision of Jewish apocalyptic for the church found its point of reference in Jesus. His divine appearing, his *Pascha* and resurrection were the eschatological something waiting to happen in the vision of Jewish apocalyptic. Because Jesus was for the church the point of reference of the Jewish eschatological vision, then a canon that contained only those writings under the "old testaments" — and that therefore contained expectations that were still "open" — could not really be closed or complete until it received those divinely inspired and apostolic writings which bore witness to Jesus Christ as the eschatological Someone whose holy *Pascha* and resurrection completed and fulfilled the expectations opened up in the "old testaments." If the canon of the Old and New Testaments now are authoritative at all, it is because they are judged by the church to bear witness faithfully and truly to the divine identity of Jesus of Nazareth and to the eschatological meaning of his incarnation.

The Christian Transfiguration of Jewish Apocalyptic

In her confession of Jesus as the eschatological Someone, the church transfigured the Jewish apocalyptic vision. If Jesus is the eschatological Someone, then the eschaton has come, or rather, it has begun. The church is given to understand that the world is now living in the Last Day of the eschaton, which began in the coming of Jesus the Christ but will not end until his Second Coming. This insight into the mystery of God's dispensation brings to the fore

an element of biblical prophecy that the Jewish apocalyptic emphasis on divine judgment had pushed to the background: The Lord
God is preeminently a God of mercy who desires not the death of
a sinner, but that he should turn from his wickedness and live (Ezek.
33:19). The delay of the Parousia, as St. Peter explains, far from
undermining the conviction that Jesus is the eschatological Someone, only confirms the surpassing mercy and long-suffering character of God as revealed in his election of Israel and in his Son's
ineffable κενωσις and condescension.

In the New Covenant — that is, in the Eucharist or in the
entrance to Christ's eschatological victory accomplished on the
cross — the righteous who love God and are faithful to his commandments may experience even now a foretaste of the victory
over death that is theirs in Christ Jesus. For to unite oneself to Christ
is to unite oneself to the One in whom all things were made and
in whom all things cohere, the One in whose image humans were
made, the One who brought Israel into being and accomplished
the *Pascha* of the first Exodus, the One who has trampled down
death by death and given life to those in the tombs by the passion
and glorification of the second *Pascha,* and the One who will execute
judgment on the earth in his Second Coming. In other words, in
Christ Jesus, all the moments of *heilsgeschichte,* both past and future,
are present so that in the offering of the eucharistic gathering, the
faithful commemorate all those things that have come to pass for
our salvation: not only the cross, the tomb, the three-day burial,
the resurrection, and the ascension into heaven, which have already
occurred in the historical past, but even his Second and glorious
Coming, which is still awaited as a future historical event but whose
eschatological reality is present in the New Testament — the eucharistic feast — of the church.

These moments of salvation history are present in the church
because they are moments that are accomplished by the Person of
Jesus Christ, who is present in the church. Not only does he accomplish them; he is the inner reality that gives them their meaning.
In Christ Jesus, the church stands within the inner meaning of
salvation history, and is thereby united to the whole of salvation
history, both those moments that have occurred in the past and
those that are yet to take place.

This eschatological principle of Christian theology illustrates the fundamental point that I want to emphasize: that what one encounters at the very heart of the life of the church is not merely a codification of apostolic teaching or a deposit of doctrines that have been handed down from generation to generation, but the very Person of the Lord Jesus Christ himself, for the tradition that has been handed down is that which was received from the Lord himself, that on the night when he was betrayed, he took bread in his hands and, having broken it and having given thanks, he gave it to his disciples, saying, "This is *my body;* this is the cup of *my blood;* do this in remembrance of *me.*"

The reality of Christ who is personally present in the church determines the identity and character of the church as the εκκλεσια. Εκκλησια is a term whose proper context is the eschatological vision of Jewish apocalyptic. Its reference in that context would be to those who have become the "elect ones" or "the chosen ones" by uniting themselves to the "Elect One" or the "Chosen One" through their participation in the New Covenant, the Eucharist. To be joined to the Elect One and to become a member of the ecclesia, the company of the elect, presupposes that one has accepted the yoke of Christ's sovereign Lordship. The rite of circumcision, however, has been perfected in the church in holy baptism, which, more than just a cutting of the skin, is a cleansing of the flesh, a union with the death of Christ and therefore a regeneration into the resurrected life of Christ. The ecclesia receives her life in the divine life of the resurrected Christ, and in that life the elect ones move and have their very being. This ecclesial society receives her character from the law and ordinances of the Lord Jesus, who taught: "You have heard it said in old times, but I say to you. . . ."

The New Covenant is the perfection of the old: the sweetness of the old that came from the Lord God who was present in the old law and its ordinances signified the possibility of an eternal life in God, but the old law by itself could not accomplish the reality that it signified. Jesus Christ, the Lamb of God, the Son of David, and the King of Israel, who took on himself the iniquity of us all and put to death in himself our death, has accomplished what the old law was all about: the overthrow of death and the enjoyment of eternal life in fellowship with God. Christ, the Second Adam, has opened the gates of Paradise; God's heavenly kingdom has broken in, the eschaton has begun. All who will may now enter; and the entrance is the church, the ecclesia, which is herself the very body and blood of the Elect One, the risen Lord Jesus Christ who is personally present among his "elect" — his church — in all his glory and power.

Conclusion: The Character and Method of Christian Theology

That Christ and his heavenly kingdom are present in the church is the fundamental conviction — or rather, experience and knowledge — of the church. This conviction determines the character and method of Christian theology. Doctrine has as its purpose to point to him who is in our midst. It is for that reason a divine teaching is filled with his presence when it is true.

Precisely because the living Lord is in our midst as a particular Person with a particular character, we are not free to let our imagination dream up "models" of God that suit our fancy or our political or philosophical prejudices. Theology is accountable not to human opinion but to the living God himself who stands as he who is who he is in the midst of the church. God himself — Father, Son, and Holy Spirit — is the source of Christian knowledge. Because he is real in himself, and because he possesses a particular character that is independent of human religious imagination, his character therefore does not change. He remains who he is, and no theological model that is more congenial to whatever is politically correct at the time, or to the latest fad in religious philosophy, can change his character: It only blinds one from seeing him *as he is*.

That this divine source is real in himself with a particular character is what necessitates and determines the ascetic character of the Christian theological discipline; for the primary aim of theological discipline is precisely to discover the true living God as he really is. This necessarily involves the ascetic struggle to move beyond all human ideas of God; to place oneself naked, as one really is, in his living presence in order to receive from him the true knowledge of himself as he really is.

The ascetic character of Christian theology transfigures it from an experiment in religious ideas to an exercise in the discipline of fasting and prayer. One strives continually to detach oneself from worldly ideas, desires, and agendas in order to attach oneself honestly to the living God as he is. The discipline of prayer and fasting is lived out daily through conscientious adherence to the commandments of our sovereign Lord Jesus Christ in the prayerful attitude of fear and humility. Inasmuch as the God of Christian theology is real, or substantive, and his acts are concrete, the ascetic discipline of Christian theology is likewise substantive and concrete. It involves fasting from food and drink and from bodily desires as the indispensable prelude to fasting from pride and arrogance, so that in both body and soul one might cultivate a living hunger for the true and living God and an inner disposition of stillness, humility, and contrition — known in Eastern spirituality as the discipline of *hesychasm* — by which one prepares oneself to receive the knowledge of God from God himself. This fast of body and soul must be completed by a fast of the mind, an exercise in κενωσις, which is a continual submission to the living Lord God in order to empty the human mind of the gods that its own philosophical imagination is so masterfully adept at producing. These idols of the intellect are lovingly produced by the subtle arrogance of the philosophical mind: From the rational principles native to the intellective faculty, it erects grand theological systems that it then idolizes as God. The deadly subtlety of this intellective idolatry is what makes theology so very dangerous when undertaken apart from the ascetic discipline of prayer and fasting and the cultivation of fear, inner contrition, and humility. For there is a particular God who is not the product of human imagination; who is real in himself and who alone has power over the living and the dead. At stake, then, is one's eternal destiny, and this is not something one ought to enjoy toying with.

The real, living presence of God the Holy Trinity in the church is the conviction that drives the ascetic discipline of Christian theology. Out of this conviction the church proclaims with confidence that God can be known as Father, Son, and Holy Spirit, and that Jesus can be known as the eternal Son of God. This knowledge is not the conclusion of some sophisticated inferential process, but the product of submitting oneself to the God of Israel who is present in the ecclesia, in his Elect One, Jesus the Christ, the Son of God.

The evangelical content of Christian theology comes from its ascetic character. To describe what one has seen and heard in the worship of the New Covenant and to bear witness to the One who is in our midst, God the Son who suffered for us on the cross and who rose again in glory and who now sits at the right hand of the Father, and who will come again to judge the living and the dead — this is the content of Christian theology.

Diadochus of Photiki, a fifth-century ascetic, summarized concisely what I have been trying to elaborate, and so I conclude my essay by appealing to the witness of this venerable saint of the church:

> The gift which inflames our heart and moves it to the love of His goodness more than any other is theology. It is the early offspring of God's grace and bestows on the soul the greatest gifts. First of all, it leads us gladly to disregard all love of this life, since in the place of perishable desires we possess inexpressible riches, the oracles of God. Then it embraces our intellect with the light of a transforming fire, and so makes it a partner of the angels in their liturgy. Therefore, when we have been made ready, we begin to long sincerely for this gift of contemplative vision, for it is full of beauty, frees us from every worldly care, and nourishes the intellect with divine truth in the radiance of inexpressible light. It is the gift which unites the deiform soul with God in unbreakable communion.
>
> Our intellect often finds it hard to endure praying because of the straitness and concentration which this involves; but it joyfully turns to theology because of the broad and unhampered scope of divine speculation. Therefore, so as to keep the intellect from expressing itself too much in words or exalting itself unduly in its joy, we should spend most of our time in prayer, in singing psalms and reading the Holy Scriptures, yet without neglecting the speculations of wise men whose faith has been revealed in their writings. In this way we shall prevent the intellect from confusing its own utterances with the utterances of grace, and stop it from being led astray by self-esteem and dispersed through

over-elation and loquacity. In the time of contemplation we must keep the intellect free of all fantasy and image, and so ensure that with almost all our thoughts we shed tears. When it is at peace in times of stillness, and above all when it is gladdened by the sweetness of prayer, not only does it escape the faults we have mentioned, but it is more and more renewed in its swift and effortless understanding of divine truth, and with great humility it advances in its knowledge of discrimination.[23]

The Christian faith is therefore kept faithfully in the ascetic character of its method. For the ascetic character of Christian theological method holds one accountable to the Person of Jesus Christ himself and to the experience of the church throughout the ages, in which the knowledge of him as Immanuel — God with us — is received and verified. The ascetic character of Christian theology means that it is wholly governed by the fear of, and the experiential knowledge of, God the Son — who is living and present in all his divinity and glory in the depths of the church.

23. Diadochus, *On Spiritual Knowledge* §§67f., in *The Philokalia: The Complete Text*, vol. 1, trans. G. E. H. Palmer, Philip Sherrard, and Kallistos Ware (London: Faber & Faber, 1979), pp. 275-76.

The Psychological Captivity
of the Church in the United States

L. Gregory Jones

By some standards, Christianity is making a comeback in American culture — including a cover story by *Time* magazine entitled "The Generation that Forgot God: The Baby Boom goes back to church, and church will never be the same." As that story indicates, contemporary Americans show a greater interest in religious matters, and large numbers of them identify themselves as believers. But many of these same people are unwilling to identify themselves as *belongers* — that is, they believe in God but the church is peripheral to their expression of that belief.

In the *Time* story, David F. Wells warns that biblical truth "is being edged out by the small and tawdry interest of the self in itself." The Christian gospel is becoming "indistinguishable from any of a host of alternative self-help doctrines." The *Time* reporter then adds that "Some of today's most influential religious figures are no longer theologians but therapists."[1]

Such a diagnosis is stunningly accurate. Even so, the therapeutic shaping of the church in the United States is both more pervasive and more pernicious than we have wanted to admit. The church's captivity to therapy is not just a reflection of the influence of James Dobson or of M. Scott Peck or of any version of the self-help/codependent/twelve-step recovery programs. Our deeper problem is that psychological language and practices have become more powerful

1. "The Generation that Forgot God," *Time*, April 5, 1993, p. 48.

97

than the language and practices of the gospel, not only in the culture but within the church. As a result, we have translated and reduced the gospel into psychological categories. Such reduction has altered and distorted the practices of the church. We have allowed it to become captive to psychology and psychological accounts of God, the world, and the nature and purpose of human life. Unlike the ancient Israelites, however, we are at best only dimly aware of our idolatry.

It is not difficult to find anecdotal evidence for distortions in the church's practices as a result of this therapeutic mindset. Indeed, some stories about various psychological banalities are quite funny, such as the famous account of "Sheilaism" in *Habits of the Heart.* Or the pastor who wears a stole that says "Don't Worry, Be Happy." Or the clergyperson who has put his Myers-Briggs type and Enneagram number on his official resumé. Or the person who has proposed that there are four Gospels in order to reflect the four different Myers-Briggs personality types. Such anecdotes are really gallows humor, however, for the consequences of this way of thinking are tragic.

That is, our psychological captivity runs deeper than humorous anecdotes, and we desperately need to address the crucial issues underlying that captivity if we are to reclaim the gospel's power to transform both our lives and the church's life. I cannot begin to provide a full account here. Even so, I want to identify, at least in broad outline, the shape of the church's psychological captivity. I do so in three parts. First, we need to recognize that, in Philip Rieff's memorable phrase, the "triumph of the therapeutic" has a stronghold on much of American culture. Second, we need also to recognize that the dominant therapeutic languages in popular American culture actually present an alternative and, in many ways, an anti-Christian account of the nature and purpose of human life in relation to God. Third, we need to reclaim the eschatological significance of the gospel in order to escape our psychological captivity. Only from such a perspective will we be able rightly to discern the significant contributions that psychology and psychotherapy might make to more faithful understandings of the gospel.

The Triumph of the Therapeutic

In his book *After Virtue*, Alasdair MacIntyre argues that every culture has within it a stock of "characters," types that furnish people with a cultural and moral ideal and that morally legitimate a mode of social existence. MacIntyre argues that modern Western societies have three such "characters": the Manager, the Rich Aesthete, and the Therapist. The Manager represents the collectivist realm of bureaucratic rationality, while the Rich Aesthete and the Therapist represent the individualist realm of private feelings and values. As MacIntyre puts it,

> The bifurcation of the contemporary social world into a realm of the organizational in which ends are taken to be given and are not available for rational scrutiny and a realm of the personal in which judgment and debate about values are central factors, but in which no rational social resolution of issues is available, finds its internalization, its inner representation in the relation of the individual self to the roles and *characters* of social life.[2]

In such a view two modes of social life are available to us: one in which the free choices of individuals are sovereign, and one in which the bureaucracy is sovereign precisely so that it may limit the free choices of individuals.[3]

Ironically, while in some respects the therapeutic and bureaucratic mindsets are antagonists, they collude to undermine the gospel and the ecclesial practices in which the gospel is embodied. Both the Therapist and the Manager see ends as given — or, more accurately, as "already chosen" — beyond the realm of their competence; each is concerned only with technique. As a result, they fail to see how their techniques reshape the ends toward which their languages and their practices are directed.

A notable instance of this is the extensive popularity, particularly within churches, of the Myers-Briggs Type Indicator. It com-

---

2. Alasdair MacIntyre, *After Virtue*, 2nd ed. (Notre Dame, Ind.: Univ. of Notre Dame Press, 1984), p. 34.

3. Ibid., p. 35.

bines the techniques of the Therapist and the Manager, purporting to be a neutral tool that identifies one's "personality type" ("I'm an ENFP") within manageable categories that can be used to differentiate those with whom one is compatible from those with whom one is not. Thomas Long aptly reveals the dangers of the Myers-Briggs in a short piece entitled "Myers-Briggs and Other Modern Astrologies." He writes,

> In short, the MBTI profiles read like horoscopes from Camelot. Taken too seriously, they can be perilously close to fortune cookies for the human potential movement. In contrast, running through the Christian theological tradition is a view of humanity that is far more complex, at once far more sober about human failings, far more truly hopeful about the human prospect, and far more infused with mystery, featuring a landscape of exhilarating peaks of communion with the holy and also valleys of tragic denial of our humanity.[4]

The Myers-Briggs is not simply a neutral technique for evaluating personality types and managing people; rather, it is an instrument predicated both on modernity's bifurcation of ends and means and on modernity's construction of the self as an enduring, discrete entity that is impervious to cultural, moral, and theological shapes.

Furthermore, therapeutic and managerial techniques fail to see how their languages and their practices are immunized against rational evaluation. MacIntyre's comments are instructive:

> The specifically modern self, the self that I have called emotivist, finds no limits set to that on which it may pass judgment for such limits could only derive from rational criteria for evaluation and, as we have seen, the emotivist self lacks any such criteria. Everything may be criticized from whatever standpoint the self has adopted, including the self's choice of standpoint to adopt.[5]

4. Thomas G. Long, "Myers-Briggs and Other Modern Astrologies," *Theology Today* 49/3 (October 1992): 294.

5. MacIntyre, *After Virtue*, p. 31.

This is as true of bureaucratic structures as it is of therapeutic ones. But while it is also an important task to focus on the former (and the correlative "Managerial Captivity of the U.S. Church"),[6] I want to focus attention on our therapeutic captivity.

Philip Rieff published *The Triumph of the Therapeutic* in 1967. This book has made a significant impact, particularly because of its prophetic critique of an emerging cultural shape in American life. Unfortunately, the subsequent twenty-five years has dulled neither its insight nor its prophetic relevance. With remarkable prescience, Rieff predicted that in a therapeutic culture there would be more of an emphasis on spirituality, not less. As Rieff described it,

> In the emergent culture, a wider range of people will have "spiritual" concerns and engage in "spiritual" pursuits. There will be more singing and more listening. People will continue to genuflect and read the Bible, which has long achieved the status of great literature; but no prophet will denounce the rich attire or stop the dancing. There will be more theater, not less, and no Puritan will denounce the stage and draw its curtains. On the contrary, I expect that modern society will mount psychodramas far more frequently than its ancestors mounted miracle plays, with patient-analysts acting out their inner lives, after which they could extemporize the final act as interpretation.[7]

But according to Rieff the effect of this psychodramatic interest in spirituality will not be a return to classical Judaism and/or Christianity, where human life is shaped and transformed in relation to sound doctrines and teachings; it will rather consist in a consumerist desire to pick and choose one's own spirituality through broad-scale experimentation. In Rieff's words, "The wisdom of the next social order, as I imagine it, would not reside in right doctrine, administered by the right [people], who must be found, but rather in

6. For an instructive discussion of these issues, see Philip D. Kenneson, "Selling [Out] the Church in the Marketplace of Desire," *Modern Theology* 9/4 (October 1993): 319-48.

7. Philip Rieff, *The Triumph of the Therapeutic* (Chicago: Univ. of Chicago Press, 1967), p. 26.

doctrines amounting to permission for each [person] to live an experimental life."[8]

This description fits not only our culture's fascination with New Age spirituality and other faddish trends; unfortunately, it also increasingly characterizes the life of the church in the United States. Thus I want to spell out in a bit greater detail several ways in which a therapeutic cancer has infected and spread throughout the church's body.

Diagnosing the Therapeutic Cancer

Important and substantive issues pertain to the relationship between psychology and theology. The gospel does not itself provide a full account of human psychology, and we need to attend to the complexities of the human psyche and human life. At its best, therapy helps us to understand the ways in which our lives are enmeshed in various dynamics of power. Further, it can help us to discern and to disentangle those dynamics — particularly in relation to the many horrifying tragedies that happen to some people. However, we need not rely only on philosophical psychology or the social sciences for such perspectives, for a classic tradition within Christianity, exemplified quite powerfully in Gregory the Great's *Pastoral Care*, attends in quite rich ways to the importance of caring for people's souls.[9]

But at its worst, and particularly in popular American culture, therapy has become a substitute for the gospel. For example, people parade themselves before Oprah, Phil, Geraldo, Sally, self-help groups, and even "church" groups in order to "share" with the world intimate and outlandish details of their "stories." These stories become more and more bizarre, including perhaps one day codependent cross-dressing adult children of alcoholics who have had strange encounters with extraterrestrial aliens. And we sit transfixed, and titillated, by such stories. But (as MacIntyre's analysis

---

8. Ibid.
9. For a contemporary appropriation of Gregory's work, see Thomas C. Oden, *Care of Souls in the Classic Tradition* (Philadelphia: Fortress, 1984).

suggests) we have no means to exercise discriminating judgment about these stories, because we lack rational criteria of evaluation. Further, we are told that such judgment might harm the people's ability to cope and hinder the development of their "self-esteem" or their attempts at "self-realization." As Christopher Lasch has recently suggested in *The New Republic,* "The only thing forbidden in our culture of exposure is the inclination to forbid — to set limits on disclosure."[10]

Such behavior creates an aura of "community," but what transpires is not reflective of the bonds of friendship. It is rather a pale, synthetic substitute, a simulacrum of community: strangers bound together by a "common" dysfunction speaking *at* one another. Even worse, the failure to recognize the importance of knowing when *not* to expose oneself verbally actually results in a collusion with sin. As Rowan Williams has suggested,

> Since the Fall, concealment is necessary and good in the sense that there is plenty in human thought, feeling, and experience that *should not* be part of shared discourse. We are alienated, divided, and corrupted; but to bring this into speech (and to assume we thereby tell a better or fuller truth) is to collude with sin.[11]

Rightly understood, confession is a central practice of Christian community; but in a culture of exposure, confession too often becomes merely another exercise in self-absorption — whether it be through pride or through abnegation.

Further, this self-absorbed "testifying" carries with it a distinctive sense of sin: there is plenty of sin to be found, but it almost always lies with others. It is society/my parents/my disease/and so forth that is/are responsible for the way I am; so I am encouraged to abdicate responsibility for my own actions. This emoting also

---

10. Christopher Lasch, "For Shame," *The New Republic* (August 10, 1992): 29.

11. Rowan Williams, "The Suspicion of Suspicion: Wittgenstein and Bonhoeffer," in *The Grammar of the Heart,* ed. Richard H. Bell (San Francisco: Harper and Row, 1988), p. 44.

trivializes important issues; when virtually any parental mistakes become "child abuse" — as has been suggested by extravagant claims about "dysfunctional" families and the origins of "codependency" — then it is impossible to distinguish the inconsequential from the serious.

Furthermore, the language of the therapeutic has created a cult of the "victim." The modern *cogito* might be better phrased "I am a victim, therefore I am." Whoever can claim the status of victim with greater authority wins, because it projects an image of innocence against which all others are somehow guilty. And the results of this are devastating. Lasch's comments are instructive: Policies based on a therapeutic model have

> given rise to a cult of the victim in which entitlements are based on the display of accumulated injuries inflicted by an uncaring society. The politics of "compassion" degrades both the victims, by reducing them to objects of pity, and their would-be benefactors, who find it easier to pity their fellow citizens than to hold them up to impersonal standards, the attainment of which would make them respected. Compassion has become the human face of contempt.[12]

Whether it be a pale imitation of community, of sin, or of compassion for victims, the therapeutic focus appears sufficiently like the gospel to seduce people into imagining that therapeutic language and categories are simply a translation of the gospel. In so doing, we fail to recognize their cancerous effects on the body of Christ.

Take Lewis Smedes's popular book *Forgive and Forget: Healing the Hurts We Don't Deserve*. Smedes is an evangelical Christian who taught for many years at Fuller Theological Seminary, and in this book he seems to be articulating a Christian perspective. After all, he indicates that forgiveness is "God's invention"; God began it "by forgiving us. And he invites us all to forgive each other." So far, perhaps, so good. But the full reference reveals its stronger links to a therapeutic mindset than to the gospel. Smedes writes that "For-

12. Ibid., p. 34.

giveness is God's invention for coming to terms with a world in which, despite their best intentions, people are unfair to each other and hurt each other deeply. He began by forgiving us. And he invites us all to forgive each other."[13]

The "hurts" and "unfairness" occur despite our "best intentions." There is no sense of the bondage of the will here, no identification of the pervasiveness of the webs of sin in which all of humanity finds itself caught apart from the gospel. We are fundamentally well-intentioned people who nonetheless are periodically unfair to others and hurt them.

As a result, the important task is my learning to forgive others who have hurt me, because the "deepest truth" about them is that they are "weak, needy, and fallible human beings."[14] I need to forgive them for my own health, regardless of issues of repentance or, for that matter, even judgments about their culpability.

Because forgiveness is linked to one's own feelings and health, Smedes thinks it is not only permissible but important to speak of "forgiving God." In his words, "Would it bother God too much if we found our peace by forgiving him for the wrongs we suffer? What if we found a way to forgive him without blaming him? A special sort of forgiving for a special sort of relationship. Would he mind?"[15] Once one makes the move to a therapeutic mindset, it becomes mind-numbingly difficult to explain why God "would mind."

The picture that Smedes presents is one in which one's psychic health replaces the goal of substantive Christian community lived in faithfulness to the triune God; in which sin is something others do to me (typically, "despite their best intentions") rather than a more complex reality that pervades our lives and relations as well as afflicts specific behaviors; and in which a false compassion without attention to issues of repentance and culpability reflects a failure to exercise a discerning judgment oriented toward graceful reconciliation.

13. Lewis B. Smedes, *Forgive and Forget: Healing the Hurts We Don't Deserve* (New York: Harper and Row, 1984), pp. xi-xii.
14. Ibid., p. 27.
15. Ibid., p. 83.

One might object that my critique fails to recognize that important insights can be learned from the social sciences in general, and psychology in particular. Further, one might object that these insights have been integrated into the discipline of pastoral care and counseling and have benefited both specific individuals and the church more generally.

While one certainly can glean such insights from psychological and psychoanalytic forms of inquiry, I would contend that analyses like Smedes's are less the exception than the rule. Further, their underlying assumptions and orientations have become institutionalized in churches, seminaries, and Clinical Pastoral Education programs. E. Brooks Holifield's *A History of Pastoral Care in America* carries the revealing subtitle "From Salvation to Self-Realization." And, while rightly appreciating the important contributions our greater awareness of psychological dynamics has made to ecclesial practices, Holifield offers the following conclusion:

> The problem is that our era has evidenced a singular preoccupation with psychological modes of thinking — modes which have tended to refashion the entire religious life of Protestants in the image of the therapeutic. When Harry Emerson Fosdick referred to the sermon as counseling on a large scale, he forgot that Protestant sermons, at their best, have interpreted an ancient text that resists reduction to the psychological. When religious educators transformed the church school in accordance with the canons of psychological relevance, they often forgot that education in the church should sometimes invite Christians to encounter a body of knowledge that satisfies no immediate or utilitarian needs. When theologians translated traditional categories into psychological terms, they often inadvertently consigned religious discourse to the sphere of the inward and private. Pastoral counseling — a counseling rightly sensitive to psychological wisdom — can best flourish when it is not exalted as the paradigm of clerical activity.[16]

16. E. Brooks Holifield, *A History of Pastoral Care in America: From Salvation to Self-Realization* (Nashville: Abingdon, 1983), p. 356.

As a result, pastoral counseling too often has been a lot of counseling with a little (and typically bad) theology tacked on at the margins. It is difficult to separate the wheat from the chaff in discussions of pastoral care, particularly because we have not yet realized the psychological captivity of the church.

But here the problem rests not so much with the people in pastoral care as with ourselves. For, comforting though it might be for us to imagine that we are the "victims" of other people's reduction of the gospel to therapy, we must take the log out of our own eye before we become preoccupied with the specks in our brothers' and sisters' eyes. That is, the triumph of the therapeutic was not simply an invasion by external forces on an otherwise healthy body; we Christians had prepared the body for the therapeutic cancer through our own distorted and distorting ecclesial practices. Most specifically, our failure to situate the church's proclamation of the gospel in relation to God's eschatological kingdom has left us in a significantly weakened and impoverished state.

A Good Servant but a Bad Master: Therapy and the Church's Eschatological Gospel

The predicament of Protestant liberalism, a phenomenon by no means limited to the heirs of the Reformation (as teaching at a Catholic college will reveal in a hurry!), is one way to identify the reasons for the church's weakened immune system. As the by now all-too-familiar story goes, Protestant liberals removed the eschatological content of the gospel, deprived the gospel of its ability to interrogate us, and transmuted the gospel into (at most) banal truisms such as "God loves you." Once these transformations occurred, the church had few defenses against the introduction of alien forces such as the therapeutic mindset. Or, more strongly put, the church no longer realized that there is something it needs to defend against.

But nagging passages in the Bible seem to run counter to Protestant liberalism's therapeutic gospel, passages that seem oriented toward Christian life embodied in eschatological community. Take the Sermon on the Mount. Richard Lischer has noted that not only does the sermon rarely appear in discussions of pastoral care, psychiatrists often turn to it for examples when discussing those features of Christianity which are "most toxic to the mental health of their patients." Lischer observes that for the psychiatrists

> the Sermon's tone violates the moral neutrality necessary for self-acceptance and change. Its obsession with purity gives free reign to the tyranny of the super-ego. The main objection to its message is that those who take it too seriously move away from the median ranges of mental health, our culture's translation of *salvus*. Far from a set of helpful guidelines for living the happy life, the Beatitudes detail the disjunction of blessedness from happiness, and salvation from health. In a society that celebrates "the narcissism of similarity" the Sermon disappoints repeatedly. What someone said of the characters in the stories of Flannery O'Connor applies to the adherents of the Sermon: "You shall know the truth, and the truth shall make you odd." The psychiatrists have a point. Theirs is no small indictment to bring against a religious program that so thoroughly dis-accommodates its adherents for a well-balanced life in a technological and therapeutic society.[17]

Lischer rightly argues that the Sermon on the Mount is an eschatological document, an expression of God's "radical pastoral care," that "can only be 'interpreted' as communities of Christians attempt to live it."[18]

The church could claim the power of the gospel, and we could be healed of our therapeutic cancer, if Christians would learn to embody such a radical pastoral care. If we are to do so, we will need to abandon the pervasive and, unfortunately, still hegemonic culture of Protestant liberalism and reclaim the eschatological focus both of the Sermon and of the gospel. But I wish it were as simple as renouncing those features of our lives and of our theologies captured by the legacy of Protestant liberalism.

17. Richard Lischer, "The Sermon on the Mount as Radical Pastoral Care," *Interpretation* 41/2 (April 1987): 164. The internal reference is to Robert Bellah, et al., *Habits of the Heart* (New York: Harper and Row, 1985), p. 72.
18. Lischer, "Sermon," p. 169.

We also need to abandon the construction of the "self" as something to which "I" have a unique and authoritative access, and that I need to "uncover" in relation to the distortions that have been inflicted on me by others/my parents/my culture/and the like. By contrast, we need to recognize anew that knowledge of the "self" is inextricably tied to knowledge of God. One way to identify these contrasting conceptions of the self is through an examination of the fundamentally different orientations of Rousseau's and Augustine's respective *Confessions*.[19] Rousseau "confesses" who he is through plumbing the wells of introspection, whereas Augustine "confesses" who he is as known by God.

In other words, rather than a therapeutic orientation — a popularized and bastardized Rousseau — toward an already-given self (or impervious "personality type") that underlies experience and culture, a Christian account ought to insist — following Augustine — on the ongoing need to construct the "self" in relation to the God from whom we have become estranged by sin — albeit a sin that we recognize only by the grace of being known by God. As Rowan Williams describes it,

> The "authentic" self is what I acknowledge as already, non-nego-tiably, caught up in continuing encounter with or response to divine action; and the acknowledgment is inseparable from con-verted behaviour. The person who knows him- or herself is manifest as such in the practice of prayer and almsgiving. Or, in short, the meaning of self-knowledge here is displayed in the performing of acts intelligible as the acts of a finite being respond-ing to an initiative of generosity from beyond itself, an initiative wholly unconditioned by any past history on the self's part of oblivion or betrayal.[20]

19. For a discussion of these issues, see Charles Taylor, *Sources of the Self* (Cambridge, Mass.: Harvard Univ. Press, 1989); Ann Hartle, *The Modern Self in Rousseau's Confessions* (Notre Dame, Ind.: Univ. of Notre Dame Press, 1983); and my own discussion of this issue in "For All the Saints: Autobiography in Christian Theology," *Asbury Theological Journal* 47/1 (Spring 1992): 27-42.

20. Rowan Williams, " 'Know Thyself': What Kind of an Injunction?" in *Philosophy, Religion and the Spiritual Life*, ed. Michael McGhee (Cambridge: Cam-bridge Univ. Press, 1992), p. 219.

That is, we only discover our "selves" in relation to the friendships and practices of the church that respond, through conversion, to God's gracious action. The healing of the self's brokenness is an unfinished and unfinishable task. As such, because our lives are inextricably bound up with one another, this task is the healing of the brokenness of not only my self but of our selves. Christian life is thus fundamentally oriented toward the coming fullness of God's eschatological reign.

As such, the gospel calls us all to a radical pastoral care. Its focus is the formation and transformation of our lives through an ever-deepening friendship with the triune God. That friendship is manifested in the friendships and practices of Christian communities in mission to the world. The goal is conformity to the image and likeness of Christ by the power of the Holy Spirit.[21]

But, one might suggest, those "friendships and practices" of the church often not only are impoverished, they also have been the occasion of colluding in the oppression and victimization of others. That is one of the reasons why Christians sometimes *need* therapy, not because of a desire to recover the tradition but to recover *from* some aspect of it. So, the interlocutor might continue, "Am I not suggesting part of the problem as the solution?"

The church's complicity in sin is, at one level, undeniably true. Unfortunately, there have been — and continue to be — impoverished and distorted convictions, practices, and communities that have gone by the name "Christian." That should not be surprising, particularly given the recognition that churches are inevitably going to be — on this side of the fullness of God's reign — holy *and* sinful communities. But what ought to be surprising is the tendency to self-deception, to a lack of penitence.

For this reason alone, the church has a place for psychological and psychoanalytic theories and practices that can help provide a check against tendencies toward deceit and self-deception. Even more, Christians can gain insights and wisdom from such theories and practices. This is particularly the case insofar as several of these theories have moved away from focusing on isolated individuals to

21. The themes of this paragraph are more fully developed in L. Gregory Jones, *Transformed Judgment* (Notre Dame, Ind.: Univ. of Notre Dame Press, 1990).

deal with larger social, cultural, and political contexts. The gospel ought not to be captured by therapy; nor ought the two simply coexist. But that is not to say that Christians cannot critically appropriate and learn from the insights of psychology and psychoanalysis.

There is, after all, a long tradition of doing so. If you grant that such texts as Aristotle's *Nicomachean Ethics* have rather rich and complex accounts of philosophical psychology, then numerous people (e.g., Thomas Aquinas) have incorporated nontheological insights about pastoral care into their theological arguments. But contemporary Christians need to take several steps in order to rehabilitate this tradition of critically appropriating and learning from the insights of psychology and psychoanalysis.

First, we need to *recognize* that the tradition exists. We need to become familiar with the strengths and limits of such notable teachers in the tradition of "pastoral care" as John Cassian, Gregory the Great, Bernard of Clairveaux, Thomas Aquinas, Teresa of Avila, and Jonathan Edwards. We also need to recognize their grounding in the gospel, their openness to insights from other sources, and the need to criticize and/or enrich their particular judgments and arguments.

Second, we need to acknowledge that the contemporary social sciences, including psychology and psychotherapy, are not theologically neutral. John Milbank has made this case concerning social theory quite powerfully in *Theology and Social Theory*,[22] but an analogous case can be made for psychological theory as well. That is, psychology as a discipline, and therapy as a practice, are not simply neutral techniques separable from ends. Their techniques are inextricably connected both to presumptions about the self and to particular desired ends. The congruence of their ends with the eschatological focus of the gospel will undoubtedly vary from theory to theory and practice to practice.[23] But if the gospel is taken to be

---

22. John Milbank, *Theology and Social Theory* (Oxford: Blackwell, 1990).
23. E.g., Jonathan Lear has instructively shown how Freud's later work might be understood in ways that resonate quite deeply with an Aristotelian (and, I would add, Thomist and more broadly Christian) perspective on human nature and destiny. Indeed in places Lear explicitly brings his analysis into

central, then the ends of the gospel will provide the criteria for rationally judging and evaluating particular claims.

Hence, third, we need critically to study and evaluate the claims of particular psychological and psychotherapeutic theories and practices from the perspective of the gospel. Robert C. Roberts, for example, has undertaken this process quite fruitfully in his recent book, *Taking the Word to Heart: Self and Other in an Age of Therapies*.[24] We should critically engage these accounts not simply for the purpose of correlating the findings of the social sciences with theological judgments, a method that continues to give too much hegemony to the myth of the "scientific" character of other modes of inquiry, but because of a love of truth and a willingness to allow our own discourses and practices to be tested by others as well as alternative forms of inquiry.

Rowan Williams has rightly suggested that therapeutic inquiry is "a good servant and a bad master."[25] For too long we have allowed ourselves to be mastered by a therapeutic mindset, and it has weakened the body of Christ's ability faithfully to witness to the gospel. Perhaps if we begin to reclaim and embody the eschatological power of the gospel, we will then be able also to see more clearly how therapy can be such a good servant.[26] Abandoning the eschatological gospel did not happen overnight; neither will we recapture it in a day. We will need long-term reconstructions of our catechesis to help us unlearn our bad habits and to learn more faithful and creative ways of eschatological living. But in the meantime, simply acknowledging that we are captives, and that we have not been singing the Lord's song in our foreign land, can begin the process of conversion that we — and the world — so desperately need.

---

conversation with Christian convictions about sin and redemption. See Lear, *Love and its Place in Nature: A Philosophical Interpretation of Freudian Psychoanalysis* (New York: Farrar, Straus, and Giroux, 1990).

24. Robert C. Roberts, *Taking the Word to Heart: Self and Other in an Age of Therapies* (Grand Rapids: Eerdmans, 1993).

25. Williams, " 'Know Thyself,' " p. 226.

26. I develop this point more extensively in my forthcoming book dealing with a recovery of Christian practices and understandings of forgiveness and reconciliation. The book is tentatively entitled *Transfiguring Forgiveness*.

Setting the Church's Agenda

James R. Crumley

To say that the church is in trouble has become almost a cliché today, a statement made in all forms of the media by the church's critics as well as by those most loyal to it. This evaluation is made of the denominations individually, with few exceptions, and is also made of the denominations together, so that it is said that, within our society, the church as a whole is in trouble.

Yet a word of caution must be spoken before this pronouncement is made. What criteria are used to measure the church's effectiveness? The criteria that are used may be a clue to the problem. They may be in terms of institutional or organizational effectiveness, such as loss or increase in membership, financial stability, growth, the solidity of the church's turf in the public sector, the church's influence in political or economic policy, the church's "image," authority, and/or whether one can trust the church as an institution. The conclusions as to the health of the church are derived from statistical studies and projections, sociological analyses, or management goals, and the ability or inability both to set them realistically and to meet them successfully. It is possible to gauge the church's performance solely in terms usually applied to organizations or social entities.

Church leadership is often cowed by such analyses, and sets out to answer such criticisms and to find solutions to stated problems from the same sociological or organizational perspectives. Thus, the reaction to a declining membership is to find ways to add more members, and to strive to make the church more attractive to whatever group is unchurched. The matter of financial constraints results in schemes to raise money and to use the most widely approved and touted techniques of the experts in the field. Leadership may strive to make the church more influential by seeking the centers of power, thus providing access to the president or to the committees of Congress or wherever those centers are presumed to be. Church leadership begins to cultivate leadership in all sectors and likes to report visits with heads of state or others who make policy decisions. The church may also attempt to build public confidence and trust in organizationally approved ways, retaining consultants or firms that are supposed to know how to build public image.

In this approach, the church becomes involved in building programs, promoting causes, and attempting to be "all things to all people." Leadership undertakes the campaign to renew and to build. Once the members have accepted the criteria of evaluation and committed themselves to the search for ways to meet the desired results, the whole church becomes involved in all kinds of activity and motion. Then the question as to how effective the proferred solutions are must be raised, because, by the time they are in place, the whole fabric that posed the problem originally has changed. In this scenario, the church appears like the proverbial tiger chasing its own tail and simply going around in circles.

Many people most loyal to the church are proponents of this approach. They insist that the church as an institution is a human organization and therefore must use the same tools and methods as any human institution. The primary question then becomes, "What works? What produces results?"

I contend for a different point of view at this fundamental starting place. The church is a human organization, yes, but at the same time it is divine, a communion of members with God and with one another. The church possesses the signs by which it is defined, word and sacrament. For this reason the primary question is not "What works?" but "How can the church be faithful?"

Therefore, we must use a different set of criteria to measure the church's vitality. The question of self-identity is paramount. What is the church, and what is it expected to be by the One who gives it? What does the Lord of the church expect the church to do? What is its mission? Such questions are in a different category from the organizational ones that I have mentioned. While it is true that the church is an organization and needs to be effective as such, its reason for being is in another, higher place. Whether the church is in trouble and in decline must be determined not primarily in terms of organizational effectiveness but in the church's being true to itself and thus to its Lord.

The greater problem today is that we are not clear about the church in precisely these dimensions. We exhibit a loss of nerve by becoming servant to everyone's expectations. We are tempted to lose the theological and ecclesiological foundations for our existence, our life, our vitality. Yet these foundations must undergird all that the church does. Even in matters such as personnel practices and policies, the church ought to act like the church and not ape the corporate model. Church structures are under both the law and the gospel of God. In the life that the church lives during the week, it must not deny what is proclaimed from its pulpit and received at its altar on Sunday. If word and sacrament "constitute" the church, then they are in the very warp and woof of the church's fabric. Any other approach divides the church into those things spiritual and those material, and that dichotomy does not work theologically for the church any more than it does for the individual person.

When we examine the documents of most mainline churches in the United States, we may find statements about the nature of the church that are theologically sound, at least according to most standards. The question is to what extent those statements are actually embodied in the other parts of the church's constitution.

Although the work of the Commission for a New Lutheran Church is now more than five years old, I want to reflect on it here, because the problems that surfaced there still plague us. Those problems arose from a pattern that was superimposed on the commission's work, a pattern pervasive in the society and in culture. All of us who were members of the commission often reflect on the process that was used and the ways in which we became "captive" to attitudes, ideas, and procedures that did not always serve us well. Much of that process and its problematic is documented in a helpful way in Edgar Trexler's

Anatomy of a Merger.[1] If errors and fallacies in human judgment could always be left in the past so that we go ahead in a different way, then all would be well and good. The poor results could be overcome. What happens, however, when we go ahead in the same way? That is the troubling question that drives much of what I am saying here.

The Constitution of the Evangelical Lutheran Church in America (ELCA) has a fine article on "The Nature of the Church." The statements on purpose are solidly confessional and describe correctly the church's mission. The difficulty is that, as the constitution was being put together, these were some of the last things to be adopted. In fact, the article on the nature of the church was adopted during the final minutes of the last meeting of the CNLC. All structural decisions had already been made, and at least one decision of crucial importance theologically, the question of ministry, was postponed because we could not agree among ourselves. Yet I do not think that we saw our disagreements as ecclesiological and that as a consequence we could not agree on the ministry that serves the gospel within the church. A task force on theology was appointed early in the deliberations of the CNLC, and, in my view, it did some of the most solid and creative work that was done during the life of the commission. Yet little discussion was held on that document, which was received as a "working document" to be used in all other decisions. However, later in the process it was clear that we did not agree on a basic ecclesiology. This document, then, did not establish the criteria by which other decisions were made.

It was then easy to assume that most issues were completely open and to be decided pragmatically. That meant that we as members were totally in control so that we could adopt church structures that we thought would work. The overarching sense of a new church also meant that we were searching for novel solutions that subjected us to the pressures of special interest groups, or to what opinion polls advised as to the wishes of the church's membership.

At least some of our present problems, reflected in most mainline churches, are the result of that approach to church and mission, a popular, widespread, pervasive point of view in our culture. This point of view requires countering, not co-option.

1. Edgar R. Trexler, *Anatomy of a Merger* (Minneapolis: Augsburg, 1991).

Lesslie Newbigin's analysis in his book *The Gospel in a Pluralist Society*[2] is most helpful. Newbegin's intention is described on the cover of the book this way:

> How does the Gospel relate to a pluralist society? What is the Christian message in a society marked by religious pluralism, ethnic diversity, and cultural relativism? Should Christians encountering today's pluralist society concentrate on evangelism or on dialogue? How does the prevailing climate of opinions affect, perhaps infect, the Christian faith?[3]

Pluralism, as Newbigin defines it,

> is conceived to be a proper characteristic of the secular society, a society in which there is no officially approved pattern of belief or conduct. It is therefore conceived to be a free society, a society not controlled by accepted dogma but characterized rather by the critical spirit which is ready to subject all dogmas to critical (and even skeptical) examination.[4]

I want to examine some aspects of our ecclesiology and their relevance in setting the church's agenda against this interpretation of culture, which I think has infected the Christian faith and the churches.

The Constitution of the Evangelical Lutheran Church in America, as I have already indicated, reflects a sound and useful ecclesiology. In fact, the appropriate basis for evaluating the program and life of the church is already intact in our governing documents. But is that ecclesiology incorporated effectively into the very life of the church? Here are only some of the pertinent paragraphs from the constitution:[5]

2. Lesslie Newbigin, *The Gospel in a Pluralist Society* (Grand Rapids: Eerdmans, 1990).
3. Ibid., cover.
4. Ibid., p. 1.
5. Evangelical Lutheran Church in America, *Constitutions, Bylaws, and Continuing Resolutions* (Minneapolis: Augsburg, 1991).

The Church is a people created by God in Christ, empowered by the Holy Spirit, called and sent to bear witness to God's creative, redeeming and sanctifying activity in the world. (4.01)

The Church exists both as an inclusive fellowship and local congregations gathered for worship and Christian service. (3.02)

This church recognizes that all power and authority in the Church belongs to the Lord Jesus Christ, its head. (5.01)

The constitution also makes an important distinction in the way in which the word "church" is spelled with a capital or lowercase "c." It acknowledges that the one, holy, catholic, and apostolic Church is not identical with the Evangelical Lutheran Church in America. While the specific terminology from Vatican II is not used, the statement of *Lumen Gentium* that the one, holy, catholic, and apostolic Church "subsists in the Roman Catholic Church"[6] is obviously intended to apply as well to the ELCA. It follows that the ELCA has given a high priority to the expression of the Church as one and to do all that it can in proclamation and program to manifest that unity, as apostolic, firmly entrenched in the tradition of faith passed on from generation to generation, as catholic, centered in both time and space reflecting its history and its universality. By viewing the church and its mission in that framework, then one sees that the Church is also holy, separated unto and deriving its life from its head, Jesus Christ.

These provisions of the ELCA describe what is often called a "high" view of the church. The church is a grace-filled gift, not a human creation. The center of the church's witness and proclamation is Jesus Christ, and the church on earth is the embodiment of that reality. That is, the church is incarnational; it is the body of Christ. This means that the life of the church as a structured or institutional unit is integral to the plan of salvation. In phrases that are perhaps more familiar to Roman Catholics than to Lutherans, the church is the "mediator of salvation" because it passes on what

6. Austin Flannery, *Vatican Council II, the Conciliar and Post-Conciliar Documents* (Leominster: Fowler Wright, 1975).

it has received from its head. In this way the church as institution has a sacramental nature, taking into its very life the promise and the gift. *Finitum capax Infinitii* — the church is also the place where that which is finite offers that which is infinite.

There is a tendency, in the United States especially, to view the church in other terms. Many who are not members of the church insist that they are believers. According to an article in *Time* magazine,

> When West Europeans drop out of church, as large majorities do, they typically lose interest in belief too, but America remains unpromising ground for atheism and agnosticism. Even most dropouts say they believe in God; though one-third also believe in re-incarnation, ghosts, and astrology. The God of their understanding is not necessarily the personal, all-powerful, and all-knowing God of orthodoxy. Nor is Jesus affirmed by boomers as necessarily the Son of God and unique Savior of humanity.[7]

The church is tempted to become relevant to the people of this culture by using their wishes and criteria rather than those of the church. Evangelism is then driven by a market or consumer-oriented mentality. The church can "meet people's needs" as people define their needs. Thus the people who may have little or no recent experience in the church develop the evaluation of the church and the church struggles to fulfill their expectations.

A recent brochure for an evangelism conference listed these workshops: "A New Look at Adult Education, practical suggestions on how to design an exciting curriculum that meets the wide range of adult needs and faith levels"; "Resources for Dynamic Music and Worship, an introduction to new worship styles and contemporary Christian music"; "Entertainment Evangelism, a look at one of the culture's top industries and how it impacts our presentation of the Gospel." As helpful to congregations as some of the discussions at such a conference may be, I am skeptical of the outcome. The church's mission is greater than meeting people's needs, as the people understand and define those needs. Again, I quote two incisive paragraphs from Newbigin:

7. "The Generation that Forgot God," *Time,* April 5, 1993.

In discussion about the contemporary mission of the church it is often said that the church ought to address itself to the real questions people are asking. That is to misunderstand the mission of Jesus and the mission of the church. The world's questions are not the questions that lead to life. What needs to be said is that where the church is faithful to its Lord, there the powers of the kingdom are present and people begin to ask the question to which the Gospel is the answer. And that, I suppose, is why the letters of Paul contain so many exhortations to faithfulness but no exhortation to be faithful in mission.[8]

The coming into the world of the promise of total salvation, of a radically new age, precipitates at the same time the appearance of those who offer salvation on other terms. Therefore it will not only be the old paganisms that fight against the church, but also the new Messianisms. Wherever the Gospel is preached, new ideologies appear — secular humanism, nationalism, Marxism — movements which offer the vision of a new age, an age freed from all the ills that beset human life, freed from hunger and disease and war, on other terms.[9]

For the church to understand the society in which it ministers is not only desirable but essential. However, for the church to allow the society to set its agenda is disastrous. The church, confident of its own identity and its mission, defines its task and develops its programs from those bases.

Two items that had a major place on the agenda for the ELCA assembly held in August 1993 were "Ministry" and "Theological Education." Some questions about ministry are in the very foundation of the church. According to the Confessions of the Lutheran Church, the church has been given the word and the sacraments, which are the source of a true and saving faith. Because the church has a primary responsibility for them, it has the ministry of Word and Sacraments. The Faith and Order document, *Baptism, Eucharist and Ministry*, speaks of the ministry as being "constitutive of the

8. Newbigin, *Gospel in Society*, p. 119.
9. Ibid., p. 122.

Church."[10] That ministry is essential; the church does not exist without it.

In this modern world, the church has other important functions, at all levels — congregational, synodical, and churchwide. We cannot imagine the church without administration, or without projects of social ministry, music, or education. Yet, important as these functions are for us, we know that the church has existed without them. To be able to distinguish between that which is essential and that which is important is necessary in order to define ministry in the church.

It was my hope that the assembly would make that distinction and would maintain the unique quality of the ministry of Word and Sacrament. The mandate for the task-force called them to consider the ecumenical dimensions of their study and of the resulting decisions. The premise assumed that the ordered ministry (in terms of bishop, presbyter, and deacon) would be considered and perhaps adopted. The ecumenical concern would likely be rather in the way the ministry of Word and Sacrament was maintained than in the terms used to describe the functions to be performed. If the church is to use the ministry of deacons, then that ministry has to be carefully defined, or both the ministry of Word and Sacrament and the ministry of the Laity are called into question.

While some of the concerns expressed here are justified in light of the debate that occurred on these issues, the final conclusions of the assembly avoided the most difficult possibilities. The assembly adopted a diaconate, but entry into it is not to be by ordination. This was the best solution, it seemed, because the definitions of that ministry and of the full-time ministers in the church who would be included were not clear. Thus, the ordained ministry is still intact in its uniqueness. However, disappointingly little was said in the report about the episcopacy, a subject that needs much discussion as the ELCA approaches full communion with the Episcopal Church and possibly with other dialogue partners.

All of this leads me to raise some questions about decision making in the ELCA. Discussions of such an issue usually relate to

10. *Baptism, Eucharist and Ministry,* Faith and Order paper no. 111 (Geneva: World Council of Churches, 1982).

the representational and participatory styles of decision making. A large assembly of approximately one thousand delegates is designed for the ELCA, and while I have not made a study of the sixty-five synods and their assemblies, I believe that many of them will have assemblies almost as large, or even larger. In a church definitely restricted in its mission by financial constraints, the expense of such gatherings ought to cause serious reflection. What percentage of the church's resources is used just in making decisions?

The nature of the church indicates that all people are not equipped to do all things. What is required for the good of the whole body depends on the gifts that are given to individuals. Thus not everyone teaches, or sings, or legislates.

Why, then, does the church need such large decision-making bodies? Is it because a smaller group would not have the same talents? I doubt it. Large assemblies have been designed with the mistaken notion that they provide for a more participatory style of decision making. Anyone with experience in such assemblies knows that this is not the case. The larger the group the less opportunity there is for members to be heard. Further, the church needs the gifts of people, gifts that are found when the people assemble, either in large or in small settings. Those gifts are not dependent on gender, race, age, or other criteria that may be similarly defined.

Furthermore, one must be cautious about using the representational principle too specifically. Delegates chosen for an assembly ought not to "represent" a certain constituency; rather, they represent the whole church. They are not to determine first of all "what the people back home" think or want, but what is needed for the life and vitality of the whole church. Nor are they to represent a specific group of people as if their interests determine what the church ought to do.

While I am not a prophet of doom, I contemplate that the financial problems of the ELCA will not be solved until a number of changes are made, among them a different style of representation and decision making. I suggest that groups approximately half the size of the present ones, brought together without regard of quotas, would make the church more effective when measured by the appropriate criteria.

Setting the church's agenda requires a focus, a concentration;

it does not imply that to be relevant the church must be shaped by the culture or society. Nor can it be all things to all people.

I conclude with two more paragraphs from Newbigin:

> Jesus manifestly did not intend to leave behind him simply a body of teaching. If that had been his intention he surely would have written a book and we should have something like the Quran instead of the book we have. What he did was to prepare a community chosen to be the bearers of the secret of the kingdom.[11]

> But where something else is put at the center, a moral code, a set of principles, or the alleged need to meet some criterion imposed from outside the story, one is adrift in the ever-changing tides of history, and the community which commits itself to those things becomes one more piece of driftwood in the current.[12]

---

11. Newbigin, *Gospel in Society,* p. 133.
12. Ibid., p. 148.

Contributors

Carl E. Braaten. Director, Center for Catholic and Evangelical Theology; Co-editor, *Pro Ecclesia;* Lutheran School of Theology at Chicago.

James R. Crumley. Bishop Emeritus, Lutheran Church in America.

J. A. DiNoia, O.P. Dominican House of Studies, Washington, D.C.; Secretariat for Doctrine and Pastoral Practices, National Conference of Catholic Bishops; Editor, *The Thomist.*

Robert W. Jenson. St. Olaf College; Associate Director, Center for Catholic and Evangelical Theology; Co-editor, *Pro Ecclesia.*

L. Gregory Jones. Loyola College, Maryland; Co-editor, *Modern Theology.*

Kenneth Paul Wesche. St. Herman's Orthodox Church, Minneapolis; Associate Editor, *Pro Ecclesia.*

Robert L. Wilken. University of Virginia; Past President, American Academy of Religion.